Fill Me Up Again

Ellen Black-Pace

The Faith Edit

Copyright © 2025 by My Heart Is In His Hands Ministry, LLC.

All rights reserved.

No part of this publication may be reproduced, distributed, or transmitted in any form or by any means, including photocopying, recording, or other electronic or mechanical methods, without the prior written permission of the publisher, except as permitted by U.S. copyright law. For permission requests, contact The Faith Edit LLC.

The story, all names, characters, and incidents portrayed in this production are fictitious. No identification with actual persons (living or deceased), places, buildings, and products is intended or should be inferred. Scripture quotations are used under common creative license and remain the property of their respective copyright holders.

Book Cover by The Faith Edit

1st edition 2025

Contents

Dedication	2
Prologue	4
Chapter 1	6
Chapter 2	18
Chapter 3	26
Chapter 4	39
Chapter 5	45
Chapter 6	58
Chapter 7	64
Chapter 8	74
Chapter 9	82
Chapter 10	89

Chapter 11	94
Chapter 12	103
Chapter 13	109
Chapter 14	120
Chapter 15	125
Chapter 16	136
Chapter 17	147
Chapter 18	160
Chapter 19	166
Chapter 20	172
Chapter 21	179
Epilogue	186
Afterword	188
About the Author	191

In Loving Memory of My Mother, Mary M. Black (1943 – 2001)
Born in North Carolina, my mother carried the strength of southern roots and the spirit of a survivor. After leaving home at an early age, she found her way to New York, and later made her home in Newark, New Jersey — where she became a pillar of faith, wisdom, and unconditional love.

She was a fighter, a nurturer, and a woman of unshakable faith. A prophet, a prayer warrior, and a teacher of the Word — a mother of eight, and a light to everyone who crossed her path.

Though life didn't always hand her the best choices, she always made the best of what she was given. Her strength raised nations inside her home, and her love became the foundation of everything I am.

They called her "Mother Teresa of the neighborhood," and it was true — she gave without counting the cost. Her laughter could break tension, her prayers could break chains, and her heart could hold the whole world.

Mama, your legacy runs through every page of this book. Your wisdom, your humor, your strength, and your love live on in me. You were a writer, a dreamer, and a woman who believed God through it all. And though the world has not been the same since you left, I know you are smiling now — proud, radiant, and free.

This book is for you, Mama. The first woman who taught me that broken vessels can still pour oil. Your daughter is still dreaming...and still believing.

— Ellen Black-Pace

Prologue

They said I was strong.
They said I was anointed.
But no one saw the cracks beneath the oil.
No one saw the woman behind the prophecy — the one who smiled on stage and bled in silence when the lights went out.
I was a worshipper without worship, a vessel poured out and never refilled. I shouted "Hallelujah" with an empty soul, and called it faith when it was really survival.
Somewhere between pain and purpose, I lost myself. The fire burned, but it burned me too.
And when the silence became too loud, I asked Him — the God I thought I'd failed, the God I thought had forgotten me — to speak.
And He did. Not in thunder. Not in miracles. But in a whisper that wrapped itself around my broken pieces:

"You are not finished. What was poured out of you, I will fill again."

That's where my story begins. Not in triumph — but in surrender. Not in glory — but in the ruins He refused to leave behind.

This isn't just the story of how I fell. It's the story of how He came looking for me in the empty places...and filled me up again.

Chapter 1

The kitchen was filled with a sweet and smoky, savory smell. Roast beef and potatoes mingled with the char of onions, creating a mouthwatering aroma. There was a fruity fragrance from the ripe strawberries and coconut that filled a mixing bowl for the cake. It promised a burst of juicy sweetness. Jenny was preparing dinner for the family. Cooking was her passion. She loved being in the kitchen but lately she had been exhausted. She hadn't felt too well. Jenny was not really up for cooking dinner, but George would have had a fit if she did not have dinner prepared.

The phone rang. It was First Lady Joyce Floyd on the other end. Jenny and the First Lady were becoming very close, but Jenny was still unsure if she should call Joyce by her first name. Joyce was the only friend Jenny had at this point. Jenny took off the apron and pulled her orange blouse down in the front.

As she answered the phone, she pulled up her khaki pants because they were falling down in the back.

Jenny struggled to hold the phone to her ear as she pulled the cake pan out of the oven, "Hello. Hi, Lady Floyd. How are you doing today?"

"Hey Jenny, you dropped in my spirit this morning." Joyce smiled as she put the cover on the pot of pasta she made for dinner. "I've been praying for you girl. What's going on?"

"Nothing at this moment. Just the same old, same old. I'm preparing dinner." Jenny placed the cake pan on top of the stove.

Joyce was not surprised at all. "Like usual...what's on the menu for tonight?"

"Nothing special. I'm just preparing a roast beef with potatoes and also cooking a small cake. Making some cornbread, that's all." Jenny said with a smile.

Joyce chuckled, "I would love to see what the 'something special' meal looks like because the nothing meal is a lot." They both laughed.

"It's really not a lot. I'm tired and feeling exhausted. I did not sleep too well last night."

Joyce, curious, asked, "Were you up praying all night? Is that the reason you haven't slept?"

"I wish! No, that's not it. Lately my prayer life has been stalled. I tried praying but I had no energy at all." Jenny poured herself a cup of coffee.

"You tried? What's going on Jenny? Have you seen the doctor? You've been feeling like this for a few months already. We talked about you going to the doctor." Joyce paused, feeling worried for her friend. "What's going on? Why do you feel this way?"

Jenny checked the roast beef and potatoes inside the crockpot. She placed the phone on the kitchen counter and put it on the speaker so she could continue to talk. "Girl, I have no idea what's going on. I try to worship. But, every time I do, something just comes up, and I get distracted."

"What do you think it is? You used to worship and pray all the time." Joyce had always admired how Jenny prayed. She often called on her to lead the prayer and worship during Bible study.

Jenny whipped the egg whites, powdered sugar and cream cheese in her mixing bowl to make her infamous cream cheese frosting for the cake. She stuck the tip of her finger inside the bowl to taste whether it was sweet enough. It was perfect. Just the way she liked it.

"I have no idea and guess what?" She covered the mixing bowl with a dish towel to wait for the cake to cool before she applied the cream cheese frosting. She took a seat at the kitchen table and reached for her bluetooth earbuds.

Curiously, Joyce whispered "What?"

"I no longer read my Bible like I used to. It's been very hard to get into it"

Joyce spoke in disbelief, "What do you mean you don't read your Word? Now you know that's a problem. You have to read your Word Jenny. That's what sustains you, along with prayer."

"I don't. I can't get in my Word. I have no desire to read or pray. I want to. I'm just tired and worn out." Immediately Jenny felt like Joyce was judging her. Maybe I should have kept that to myself, she thought.

Joyce explained "Then you have a desire. If you want to, then that's a desire. You need to see a doctor, young lady. The fatigue is getting worse. It's probably interfering with your study time and prayer life."

"Huh?! What do you mean I have a desire?" Jenny heard what Joyce was saying but didn't see what the doctor had to do with her prayer life.

Joyce attempted to make it as clear as possible, "You said you don't have a desire. But, you do because you want to pray and read. That's a desire. You just need to tap into it."

"Oh wow! I didn't see it like that. And yes, the fatigue is getting worse. I promise I'll make a doctor appointment soon." Jenny realized she lost a few pounds and that her hair had gotten thinner. She rose and walked to the counter, checking whether the cake had cooled enough for frosting. She hovered over the cake, fingertips brushing the edge. Still warm. Not yet ready. The frosting would have to wait.

"There's nothing wrong with your spirit man," Joyce explained. "It's your flesh that's acting up. I believe fatigue has a lot to do with it. The flesh won't allow you to worship because you are not feeling well."

"Wow! How do I get the flesh from acting up? I used to fast in the past. I fasted a lot. But now, I have problems doing that." Jenny was out of breath. She took a seat at the kitchen table.

"It's all about discipline. You have to discipline yourself and get your flesh under control. I do believe once you start feeling better physically you will start reading your Bible and praying again. You shouldn't fast while you are weak, Jenny. I don't advise that. That wouldn't be good at all."

"How do I go about discipline? I tried before. How did I get to this point when I used to worship, pray and read my Word constantly daily?" Jenny ignored the statement about seeing a doctor. She was more interested in getting answers for her prayer life and fasting. She kept telling herself all she was missing was sleep and she would be better. Fasting and prayer helped her in the past and Jenny felt that was all she needed. She was expecting worship to help with how she was feeling.

Joyce knew Jenny was ignoring her advice about seeing the doctor. "You have to seek the Lord for that. Ask the Lord about it. And go see the doctor, Jenny."

"Thanks, First Lady. I will just do that." Jenny looked over at the cake.

"Anytime. I'll call you later. Jenny please make sure you call the doctor and make an appointment before the week is out. Promise me you will do that."

Jenny made a promise to Joyce, "Yeah, I will. Ok, speak to you. Love you."

Jenny Jenkins was a hard-working woman. She was a worshipper who loved the Lord and desired to do his will. She was a people pleaser, but wanted the Lord to deliver her. She knew she couldn't keep doing things the way she was doing them.

George caught sight of Jenny in the bedroom. She was lying on the king-size bed, surrounded by pillows. Jenny wore blue silk pajamas and her hair pulled back into a ponytail, her usual hairstyle lately. George would have missed her if she hadn't moved. He thanked God he didn't enter the room. He tried to turn fast to leave because he did not want to see her. Lately, all she did was bitch and complain. George was not up for it today.

Jenny looked up from the book she was reading on communication and saw George trying to sneak back out the room. She could tell by his body language that he was not in the mood. But, she refused to allow this opportunity to pass. She noticed he had his locs re-twisted and shaped up since the last time she saw him. He was wearing a different dress shirt than he had on earlier. Instead, he had a green and purple striped shirt with green dress pants. He looked so handsome standing there with his gator dress shoes matching the colors he was wearing. He was a stylish dresser and took wonderful care of himself. She could see George's muscle coming through the tight shirt he was wearing. For a second, she felt prideful to have such a handsome husband.

Jenny, determined to use some of the tools she just read in her book, spoke to George, "Hey, honey."

George rolled his eyes at Jenny, "Hey." He came all the way into the bedroom.

"How was your day?" Jenny kept the conversation going to test to see if he was okay.

George snapped at Jenny, "The same as it was yesterday. Do you really care?" George pretended he was looking for something to distract Jenny so he opened the top drawer to the dresser. Maybe he could get her not to ask so many questions. It didn't work.

Jenny looked at him and bit her lower lip. "What are you looking for? Maybe I can help you find it." Praying that his mood didn't switch from not wanting to talk to wanting a blowout argument. George didn't respond. He walked over to the nightstand and then over to the closet without responding.

"What are you looking for, honey? Jenny sat up in bed. She was hopeful that she could get a few words in before George did. He usually went off in a rant just about everyday now.

"Don't worry about it. I don't need your help. Look, I'm not in the mood for a bunch of questions." George slammed the closet door causing the door to reopen.

"I was just asking you what you are looking for. I might be able to tell you where it is." She said, shaking her head.

"You probably can...you are always moving everything. You don't know how to keep your hands off my stuff." George sat on the bed far away from Jenny. He smelled the body lotion Jenny had on. She smelled like strawberries and mango, his two favorite fruits. He closed his eyes for a moment to take in the fragrances. Jenny's next question took him straight out of the trance.

Jenny knew that George was trying to ignore a conversation but she didn't care, "George, I think we need to talk. We can't keep going on like this."

"Didn't I just tell you, I do not feel like talking?" George threw up his hands. He went back over to the top drawer, pulled out a pile of paper and looked through them.

"No. You said you were not in the mood for a bunch of questions. I just asked you one question."

George looked at Jenny and said "and talking...I do not feel like talking. I did say that." He sank back onto the bed, unaware he had sat close enough for Jenny's hand to brush against him.

Jenny was getting upset now. "You did not say that. What you said was you weren't in the mood for a bunch of questions. You didn't say anything about talking."

"I'm saying it now." He looked at her sideways. "You do understand that right. No questions...no talking."

"I miss you, George. I miss what we used to have together." She ignored what he said and tried to touch his hand but he pulled back.

George looked at her sideways, got up from the bed and moved across the room to the file cabinet they had in the corner. The smell from the body lotion Jenny had on caused a fruity wind to spread throughout the bedroom. He almost grabbed Jenny and put some good loving on her. She knew he loved body lotion but he refused to be trapped in her webs tonight. He had things to do.

"I miss you, I need some attention, George. I am all alone. You are never here. We don't spend time with each other anymore. I'm lonely George." More hurt than angry, Jenny pleaded with George.

"Dawg, where is that paperwork?" George needed the contracts he had his lawyers to draw up about adding another building for the warehouse. Getting frustrated about the missing paperwork, he slammed the door on the file cabinet. He went back and forth across the room, digging through piles and tossing things aside until he found the papers.

"Look, I'm tired, Jenny." George really did not have time to get into it.

Frustration began to rise up in Jenny. She clenched the book she was holding "From what, George? Maybe if you come home, you can get some rest. All you do is come eat breakfast, lunch and dinner. Then you go out again after each meal. You reappear early in the morning, walk in late for lunch and then grace us for dinner."

Without looking at Jenny, George stated "That's a question, Jenny, and I said I'm not in the mood for questions. Look, I do come home and I sleep on the couch." He lied.

"Most nights I just sleep there and leave before you get up. I told you I have a lot going on with the company that requires me to work long hours. You can't run a 24-hour trucking company at home all the time. Problems happen and I need to be there to take care of them. I told you this several times. Even Rick explained this to you. What more do you want me to do?"

Jenny began to cry out of anger. She knew George was lying about work. He was just trying to ignore having a conversation with her. George changed his tone because he realized the only way to get out of the tough conversation was by sounding nice.

"I am exhausted and busy," he said through clenched teeth.

Jenny refused to give up, "It's been a month already, George...a month. I'm frustrated and tired. All my responsibilities include cooking, cleaning and attending to these kids. I work in this house twenty-four hours, seven days a week. I take on all your secretary work and tend to your momma. I don't get a break."

George was trying to stay calm but it was not working, "And let's not forget church, prayer, worship and your church folks. You put a lot of time in down there at that devil den. Maybe, if you pull back from that you won't be so tired. I know it will save me a lot more money too."

George Jenkins was an excellent provider for his family. He was upset because Jenny started to attend church. He felt like she left him out, but pride would not allow him to admit that. George's anger came from feeling neglected and rejected, not just from Jenny. George had felt rejected from his dad who was no longer living.

"George! Why would you say that? One day, you will learn to keep your mouth off of God's people. You say things that are not true and only to justify your wrong. You just place the blame on someone else." Jenny got up from the bed and placed the book she was reading on communication on the nightstand.

"If you let go of that church stuff, maybe you won't be so tired. It's doing nothing for you, for us or most important for our family, anyway."

"George, take that back. Don't speak against God. Please do not do that. Take that back!" Tears began to run down Jenny's cheeks. She could see the smoke coming from his nostril and immediately recognized the spirit behind his comment.

George looked at her with disgust, "Ever since you've been in this church business, all you do is cry. I'm tired of that. You are so soft now. Where is the tough Jenny I used to have? Look, I gotta go. I do not have time for this." George walked out as his phone rang.

George answered his phone once he left the bedroom. "Hey baby. Didn't I tell you I would call you back once I got in the car? Sometimes, you just don't listen."

Chapter 2

The thump of a basketball echoed against the back porch patio before the door swung open. Johnny bursted into the kitchen like a whirlwind with his headphones blaring Tupac's "All Eyez on Me." His head bobbed to the beat as he rapped every lyric, spitting bars with a grin that made it clear he felt untouchable.

He spun the ball on his finger, let it roll down his arm, and caught it behind his back before tossing it on the counter next to his book bag. He took off his brown jacket and threw it onto the end table in the family room.

"Momma! Momma!" he called, half-rapping, half-shouting, his voice swallowed by the music in his ears, Johnny didn't hear Jenny yelling out to him.

From down the hall, Jenny's voice shot back, sharp and tired. "What?" she yelled from her bedroom.

Johnny barely heard her. He yanked open the refrigerator, scanning the shelves for anything quick to eat, still nodding to the beat.

"Momma, where are you at?" he hollered again, louder this time, drowning out everything else.

Jenny came running out of the bedroom thinking something was wrong because Johnny was yelling at the top of his lungs. She stubbed her big left toe on the end of the kitchen table, the pain went through her left foot causing her to curse out in pain.

Hopping on her foot, she yelled at Johnny, "What! What John John? She touched his back causing him to jump, almost dropping his phone."

"Momma, you didn't hear me calling you?"

"You didn't hear me answering you?" She slapped him on the back of his head and limped over to the fridge bumping Johnny out the way. Jenny took apple juice from the fridge and grabbed a glass from the cabinet to pour herself something to drink.

Johnny watched as his mother prepared the drink and took the glass out of her hand as soon as she was done. "Thanks and no, I didn't. What is wrong with your foot?" Johnny asked as we walked over to the couch. He flopped on the couch being careful not to spill his newly acquired beverage.

"Maybe you could hear, if you take these things out of your ears," Jenny walked over to her son and pulled the headphones out of his ear.

"I stubbed my toe on the end of the table. What do you want, John John? I was watching my show before you rudely interrupted me."

Jenny sat down next to her son on the couch eyeing her drink in his hand. The pain in her foot lifted some. Johnny leaned in to plant a kiss on his mother's cheek and laid his head on her shoulder with puppy dog eyes.

"I need fifty dollars."

Jenny pushed Johnny's head off her shoulder and looked at him sideways. "Fifty dollars for what?"

Johnny laid his head on his mother's shoulder once again trying to be convincing. "For a fitted." Johnny blinked those big greenish brown eyes at his mother. He continued to smile at her with puppy dog eyes but it didn't work on Jenny.

Paula stepped into the kitchen from the side sliding door, a book bag slung over her shoulder. Johnny's twin paused just inside the doorway, catching his words.

"Fifty dollars? For that big head?" she said, smirking. "Boy, that head needs a building permit."

Johnny shot her a look and grinned. "My head is perfectly proportioned for greatness."

Paula dropped her bag onto a chair and headed for the pantry. She pulled the cabinet open, scanning for a snack. She grabbed a bag of Doritos, and flopped into the nearest chair.

"Yeah, greatness at wasting money," she said around a mouthful of chips, her eyes flicking between Johnny and her mother, curious if Jenny would give in this time.

"Fitted? What's a fitted boy? You have plenty of belts. You do not need another one."

Johnny took a sip from his glass of apple juice, "A hat, mom, a baseball cap. "You know momma, it's the latest style." He pulled out his phone to show his mother a picture of the hat he wanted on Google.

"John John, you must be crazy if you think I'm about to give you fifty dollars for a hat." Jenny got off the couch to go pour herself something else to drink. She realized the pain in her foot was gone and sighed to herself in relief. Thank God she didn't break it.

Paula smirked, crunching another chip. She waited to see what Johnny would try next.

"Why? Mommy, please. All the cool kids at school have one. It's only fifty dollars."

"Child, didn't your dad just give you two hundred dollars? Where is that money?" She sat at the kitchen table. "John John get your book bag off the kitchen counter."

Johnny stuck his right foot out "That money is on my feet. The new Air Jordan just got released. They were two hundred and fifty dollars. Come to think of it...I need a hundred. Fifty dollars for the fitted and the other to pay my homeboy back for letting me borrow fifty."

Jenny looked at Johnny sideways and focused on his latest fashion purchase. Confused, she said, "You should have bought last year's Jordans for a hundred and fifty dollars and taken the other fifty to buy yourself a fibit. Because if you think I'm about to give you fifty dollars for a fibo, you are buggin'."

Johnny looked at his mother jokingly, "A fitted mom. And I got last year's Jordan. I can't wear the same style of sneakers for two years in a row, Mom. What would the ladies think?" Johnny removed his backpack off the kitchen counter and picked up his jacket from the end table.

Jenny did not care, "Fibit. Fibo. Fitted. Whatever it is, I'm not giving you fifty dollars for no hat. You don't have to buy every pair of Jordan that comes out, John John."

"Mom, yes I do. I got to keep up with the latest fashion. My women love for me to look flesh and fly," Johnny spun around in a circle.

Jenny laughed, "Really? Then you need to ask them for fifty dollars."

Johnny shook his head, "I can't have them thinking I'm broke, Mom how would that look?" He pulls a chair out and sits next to her at the table.

Paula grabbed another bag of Doritos from the pantry, swung her head around, and smirked. "Boy, please. You are broke. And the ladies already know."

Jenny laughed "I agree you are broke, you don't have any money. You are not getting fifty dollars from me to buy a fibit."

"A fitted mom. Say it with me, FITTED." Johnny placed both hands on her cheeks and tried to move her mouth.

She smacked his hand away from her face, "Say, I don't have any money, Say it with me." She chuckled out loud.

Johnny looked around the kitchen and nook area. He admired the fine furniture and the expensive kitchen gadget on the counter. The new Samsung refrigerator his parents purchased was a talking fridge with tv and bluetooth. He knew they had the money. So he tried another approach to get the money from his mom.

"Oh, but you see. I look at it like this. I'm only 16 ½ years old. You and dad have to provide room, board and food along with clothes until I reach 18. Until then, whatever is yours and dad belongs to me. That's the law."

"Oh really, that's how you see it? Are you sure about that?" Jenny got up from the table to place the empty glass into the sink. She returned and sat across from John John.

"Yeah, that's how I see it. He shook his head yes, Yep that's how I see it." Determined to get his point across, Johnny folded his arms across his chest.

Jenny got up from the kitchen, went over to the kitchen drawer and pulled out a pile of paper. She laid them in front of Johnny.

"What's this?" Johnny looked through the pile of papers and realized they were bills. Wondering why his mother would hand him the bills, Johnny threw both hands in the air.

"This here my son is me and your dad bills, oh my bad and yours too. You said it yourself, what your dad and mine are yours as well. Well here are the bills for this month. That we have to pay..Meaning you, me and your father." Jenny smiled knowing she just won the debate.

"Mom, you're bugging, you cannot be serious, right." He pushed the pile of bills away from him and gets up from the table.

Jenny shook her head and bursted out laughing. She noticed the brown jacket Johnny had was also new. A Sergio Tacchini double zipper and sleek. She had to admit Johnny was stylish. He knew fashion but Jenny was not giving him any money. She wished he would learn how to budget and stop spending so much.

"Mom, come on, you know what I mean." Putting his glass into the sink and turning to his mother and saying, "Mom, I did not mean everything you have."

"NO! You said it yourself" Jenny picked up the pile of paper and waved them in Johnny's face, "These belong to you too. And I expect you to pay them by the weekend." Jenny gathered the papers and pushed them toward her son.

Johnny pushed the papers out of his face as Jenny walked away yelling over her shoulders. "I'm not playing with you this weekend."

Jenny walked out the kitchen back into her room and started to laugh again. Paula crunched a chip, leaned back in the chair, and grinned. "Ooo, she got you," she teased. "Better start selling those Jordans. Want me to set up a GoFundMe for you?"

She grabbed her book bag from the chair, still laughing, and headed toward her bedroom.

"Man she buggin' if she thinks I'm paying bills. I don't have a job and I ain't got no money. They got a lot of bills and they are the ones with all the money. They can pay their own bills." Johnny got up, bounced the ball and left the papers on the table. He put his headphones back in his ears and left out to play basketball with his friends.

Chapter 3

A large burgundy leather couch sprawled across the center of the living room. A large, flat-screen TV dominated the wall above a cluttered entertainment center. The cabinet overflowed with old DVDs and a collection of family photos. Several large windows to the back garden let in natural light. The natural light beamed down into the newly remodeled pool house George just had the work done to recently. The family room was the preferred entry to the house; it was the closest to George and Jenny's bedroom. They preferred it this way so they could monitor the twins. The back of the house entry also led into the newly remodeled French kitchen, and a much shorter walk to everyone's bedroom.

Paula came into the house on the phone as she put away the clothes she changed into. "I got to go, I'll call you later. I'm in the house now." She walked into her room and pushed the clothes down in her hamper. She jumped when her father entered the room and caught her by surprise.

George and his long-time friend, Rick, entered. Rick bumped shoulders with Paula and she shoved him right back.

"Hey Runt!" Rick slapped Paula on her back. She swung at him but he jumped out of her reach. Paula dipped the other direction and hit him. Before Rick could react, she acknowledged her dad.

"Who are you calling a runt, peanut head? Hey daddy," Paula leaps up and gives her daddy a kiss on the cheeks.

"Hey Diamond. What's up? And why didn't you answer your phone, I was calling you." George kissed her on the forehead. "You had me worried when you didn't answer your phone, Diamond."

"Yeah, he was calling you!" Rick gave Paula the eye.

"I was at school or in the car with the radio loud. I did not hear my phone."

"You're not driving while on the phone, are you? I told you about texting and driving. You know what happened last time. I can't afford another one of your accidents."

"No Daddy, I promise you. I'm more careful. That's why I did not answer my phone while I was driving."

"Your car has Bluetooth, young lady. You should answer your father's question. Why didn't you answer your phone? You had us both worried about you when we called you."

"I did...I just said I was at school or in my car. Calm down Uncle Rick. You act like you are my father. You just play my uncle."

"Ok, all right. I'm more than that, I'm your protector along with your Dad. You understand."

"You are asking me more questions than my father. You are not my daddy. Calm down! I'm home now and you can see I'm safe and sound."

"Okay...still, answer your phone so we won't be so worried."

George loved how Rick was just as overprotective as he was. "Uncle Rick is just concerned about you Paula. There is so much going on. Next time, just answer your phone. Where is your mother at?"

George walked out of Paula's room and looked around trying to see where Jenny might be.

Paula followed him out into the living room on her phone not looking up. She answered her father, "I don't know. I think she might have taken a nap. Her car is outside, so she is definitely here."

George peered into the bedroom. Jenny was fast asleep. George thought to himself, *Thank God because I don't have time for a bunch of questions.*

The tall man emerged from the bedroom to talk to Rick, "Jenny's asleep. Let me take a quick shower before she wakes up. I won't be long. Rick, relax and stay out of my fridge. Be very careful, Jenny is asleep."

"Relaxing is what I will do. Staying out of the fridge is what I will not do. The way your wife cooks, boy. You should be glad I'm not here every day." Rick said as he licked his lips at Paula.

"It seems like you are." Paula licked her bottom lip back at Rick. "Don't you have your own home to go to?"

"I'm not playing Rick. That roast beef is tomorrow's lunch for me and stay away from it."

Rick walked to the fridge and opened the door. "That's an invitation, bro. Thanks for letting me know it's in there." Rick pulled the roast beef out of the fridge along with mayo and bread to prepare himself a sandwich.

"Rick, I'm not playing with you." George said as he went into the other room. Rick ignored George and continued to make his sandwich.

Paula sat on the couch. Rick checked if George entered the bathroom and then he waited for the water. He checked to see if Jenny was awake. Then Rick returned to the couch with the sandwich he made. Rick quickly ate the sandwich as the tension between him and Paula got bigger and bigger.

"Thank God, I don't know how long I can put up with this." Rick pulled Paula close to him as he finished his food.

Paula got up and straddled herself on Rick's lap, started kissing him and whispered, "I want us together more often."

Rick was a very handsome man, his broken Jamaican slang along with Spanish made him so sexy to Paula. He was not as muscular as her father but Rick's muscles and the smell of his Dolce Gabbana cologne turned her on.

"I can't wait until I turn 18. I'm out. I only have 1 ½ years to go."

"Yes, age ain't nothing but a number. Your body says something else to me. I can't get enough of you. You got me sprung girl." Rick rubbed Paula's butt. "But, you are delusional if you think your parents will allow us to be together after you turn 18. That will never happen."

"You know, my daddy would kill you if he knew you were tagging his little girl." Paula bit Rick's bottom lip.

"Little girl, grown woman, girl! The way you make me feel...that's some adult stuff right there. You better start answering your phone before you make me go crazy out here. I feel like I'm losing complete control."

"Calm down, I had to wash off from our afternoon rendezvous. I couldn't come home smelling like your house. You know my mother has the spirit of discernment. She picks up everything. You don't want that at all. You know Mommy is crazy."

"Her discernment is off, because she hasn't picked up this right here." Rick kissed her. "You left my house on your school lunch break. Where have you been since then?"

Paula pulled back and got up off Rick's lap. She sat next to him instead. Paula picked up something. She didn't know what it was but she figured it was time to tone it down. "We have to be careful because I can't let anything interfere with all this." Paula pointed at Rick's private parts.

"I feel like a grown woman when you are inside me. It comforts me, it gives me joy."

Rick was not the only person that gave her pleasure. Paula was also seeing Steve and other boys. She kept her options open. Steve was the high school quarterback and the star of the football team. Paula was using Rick to get what she wanted from him. Her boo thing was Steve. Rick was too old and she wanted someone much younger who could handle her sex drive. Steve could hang. Rick was good only when he took the blue pill.

As she put on a good act, Rick pushed her away from him. "Your father is coming. The water just turned off."

Rick had always been afraid of George since they were younger. But, when it came to Paula he was weak. Rick tried his best to end the affair. Every time he tried Paula blackmailed him. She would entice him with sex to keep their arrangement going. Rick knew it was wrong. He felt like a pervert having sex with Paula. He was so caught up though. It was hard for him to let go.

Paula came onto him one night when he crashed at George's house because he was drunk. He was thinking it was someone else because he was intoxicated. She did things to him no grown woman ever did. By the time Rick knew it was Paula that night, it was too late. The day after Paula snuck and had sex with him, Rick vowed never to touch her again. But Paula got into his head and he was stuck and couldn't get enough. Rick knew he was wrong and could go to jail, but the girl had a spell on him.

Jenny walked into the living room. She looked at Paula and Rick and shook her head. Paula jumped up

"Hey mom." She ran to give her mother a kiss.

"Hey, baby." Jenny hugged Paula while eyeing Rick.

Paula was so beautiful. She favored Jenny so much. She was the full package of body and looks. Jenny knew Paula was no longer a virgin. She asked and Paula admitted she wasn't. George would have been so upset with Jenny if he knew she took Paula to the doctor to get on birth control. She didn't want Paula to become a teenage mom like she had.

"How was your nap? You were sound asleep. Are you still not feeling well?"

"My nap was short." Jenny looked at Rick. "I had a dream. Want to know what my dream was about Rick?"

Jenny ignored Paula's question about how she felt and moved closer to Rick.

"No, not really. I'm really not all that interested in it." Rick looked away from Jenny. Sometimes she could be scary. Rick did not trust Jenny at times.

"It was about me killing this snake. The funny thing about the snake, it had a human head. I didn't recognize who the head was at first. But as I was about to examine the head of the snake I-"

Rick interrupted Jenny. "George! George! Hey George!" He jumped off the couch

George yells back "Yeah, I'm coming out now. What's up?"
Rick looked at Jenny, "How long will you be a man?"
"Be out in a few."

Paula laughed because she knew her mother could seem a little crazy. Everyone knew the old Jenny and how dangerous the old version of her was. They used to call her, "Jenny from the block." And for bad reason, too. Paula heard rumors about her mother and saw her mother in action before she got in church. Rick had every reason to be scared of her mother.

Paula's phone rang and she picked it up. Her best friend, Judy, on the other end waited to get some good gossip about what happened earlier.

"Hey girl! What? Wait, let me go to my room. Love you, Mommy. Talk to you later Uncle Rick."

Judy was the only person that knew Paula was messing around with Rick. Judy envied Paula, not only because of her looks and banging body but because of how confident Paula was. Judy had an older boyfriend, but not as old as Rick. Her boyfriend was just five years older. Rick gave Paula anything she wanted because Paula kept threatening to tell her father. Every time Rick gave in to the blackmail. But Paula would never tell because telling her dad about Rick would expose her. Rick was just too stupid to realize that.

"You never called me back. What happened when you got home?"

"Nothing, I threw the pregnancy test away into the dumpster." Paula began to put away the laundry that her mother asked her to fold several days ago.

Looking around the room Paula thought to herself, *Maybe I should redo my bedroom. At least the color.* The pink was too girly. She needed a more mature color now. Everything in the room was either pink or white. Paula looked under her bed to the lingerie chest she had hidden. She opened it up to examine the lingerie Rick just purchased her.

She agreed with herself that she needed to redo the color in her bedroom. Paula was no longer a little girl but a grown woman. At least, that's how Rick and Steve made her feel. Paula turned her attention back to Judy and threw the rest of the lingerie onto the bed. She flopped on her king-sized platform bed and bounced up in the air. Paula giggled to herself and realized just how spoiled she was.

Judy was absolutely astounded how many times Paula dodged the pregnant bullet. "You once again escaped another pregnancy scare girl. You are one lucky nut."

"Yeah right, I am but I don't know what's going on. I haven't gotten my period in the last two months and I've been feeling like crap lately." If Judy really knew how scared Paula felt maybe she wouldn't look up to her as much.

"How many tests did you take again, like ten right?"

Paula sighed a little, "More like twelve. Rick brought seven himself once I told him I didn't get my period last month. He almost had a heart attack. You should have seen how he was acting. He makes sure we use a condom ever since."

"You still don't know what is going on with you." Judy shook her head and noticed that Paula was feeling a little down. She was sure that Paula was pregnant and was concerned. Judy was the one to suggest Paula take a pregnancy test. Judy was the only friend Paula had at school and their friendship meant a lot to her.

"At this point I do not care as long as it's not a baby. That will be so odd to have a baby come out looking like Rick. I'll be on the Maury. Who's the baby daddy?

They both busted out in laughter. Judy laughed and jokingly said "You are not the father! At this rate, you wouldn't know who the father is…Rick or Steve you would be confused at this point. You do both of them sometime in the same day."

"Most likely it will be Rick because Steve does not play. He made it very clear about not becoming a father before he gets drafted to the NFL, so we definitely use protection. We have to, we are humping like bunnies."

"Girl, I do not know how you do it. Don't you get tired?"

"Rick doesn't last as long as Steve. It's usually twice and he is done. Unless he pops that blue pill! Then, it's on and popping. I make sure those are around when Steve is not available."

They both laughed.

"But for real, I'm not feeling 100%. I will probably try to go to the doctor. I feel like I have the flu or a cold. Maybe they can tell me why my period is on vacation."

"Yes, please! Go get checked because I can't catch the flu or cold because of you. I have a hot weekend coming up and I can't afford to get sick. You coughing, too! Yeah, you need to go handle that. Get some antibiotics quick and hurry."

"Yeah you might be right. Girl, I'm about to jump in the shower. I gotta get Rick and Steve off me. I'll talk to you later."

"Okay, talk to you later!"

Before they can hang up Judy says, "Paula, I am praying for you."

Meanwhile Jenny was looking at Rick up and down on the couch. Rick had taken a seat back on the couch on the far end. Jenny moved in a little closer. Rick stared at her with a curious look.

"There's something about you I don't like. You are sneaky, and when it comes to my daughter, I don't trust you. I smell flesh all around you. You better pray to God I don't find out what it is."

"What you are thinking Jenny is all wrong? There's nothing between me and Paula. You have a twisted mind; she is like my own niece."

"Why would you say that? I said no such thing."

"It's what you are thinking." The sweat began to form, Rick wiped his forehead with the back of his hand. He was feeling very uncomfortable and afraid his cover was about to be blown. Jenny noticed Rick was sweating and moved a little closer to him.

"How do you know what I am thinking, huh? I never once said anything was going on with you and Paula but-"

Rick interrupted her again, "Go ahead, man. You crazy." He got up from the couch, picked up the remainder of the roast beef and sat back down on the smaller chair near the back door.

Jenny noticed how very uncomfortable Rick was and she pressed the issue.

"You haven't seen crazy yet. Your life will lack purpose if I uncover anything. Listen, I do not think you and Paula are messing around with each other. I believe you are covering up for her. As her uncle, I feel you should make it your business to act like her uncle rather than a friend. If I uncover anything and I find out later you knew about it, that will not be so pretty for you."

"Man, you think I'm crazy? George would kill me. Paula is only 16. She is like my niece. I have been in her life since birth. She is young enough to be my daughter. You really need to chill and get more rest because you sound crazy and acting crazier." Rick burst out laughing

Jenny pulled out a pocket knife. "It's not George you have to worry about. I'm warning you to stay away from my daughter. There's something about you I don't like. Believe me if I thought something sexually was going on between you two I would have put this knife so far up your ass it would take a surgery to remove it. Do you understand me, Uncle Richard?"

Rick jumped off the couch. "We used to be close Red. What happened to us? We used to be very close friends. I don't understand you. Once you started having a problem with George, you started taking it out on me as well. What did I do to you? I have nothing to do with how George treats you but for some reason you believe that I do."

Jenny smirked at him, "You turned sneaky. There is something about you and my daughter. I pray to God I'm wrong. But if I'm not, only God will help you because heaven will be waiting."

"You keep saying this crazy shit. There is nothing going on between me and Paula. Man you are crazy for even thinking such a foolish thing. You just said you don't think anything sexual is going on between me and Paula. Now you're here saying this wack shit to me again."

"Ready to go?" George walked into the room. Jenny put the knife away. George looked at both Rick and Jenny and could tell something had taken place between the both of them. "What's going on with you two?"

Rick wiped his forehead. "Nothing. Yeah man, ready."

Rick has been a best friend to George since childbirth. Their parents were best friends. Rick had been in a sexual relationship with Paula since she was 13 and a half. He knew how wrong it was, but he couldn't get enough of her. Besides, she came onto him first.

Chapter 4

Jenny sat in the church waiting for her pastor, Jamal Floyd, to say something she could grab onto because of the week she had. She was running late for church that Sunday because George came home early in the morning demanding she run his bath and iron out his clothes. George didn't even have the nerve to say, "Thank you," afterward.

Jenny no longer recognized the man she was married to. George was mean and evil. He has no respect for her. *What did I do for him to hate me so much?* The question echoed in her mind as she sat on the edge of the bed the night before. Jenny was spent. After running George's bath and ironing his clothes, she barely had enough strength to get dressed herself.

Earlier that day, Jenny had let her body fall back against the bed. Less than an hour was left before church but she was drained, bone-tired. Jenny's heart still longed to make it to church, to sit in the sanctuary and hear the Word. So she pushed herself to get there. As she pressed her way, Jenny began to have a conversation with herself. "I promise I'm going to the doctor this week. I can't do this any longer, I barely can move."

The lady sitting next to Jenny hollered, "Amen," causing her to jump out of her thoughts recalling the morning. She looked around and saw the church had fallen into pure worship. "How I miss the presence of God and I need all of this," Jenny began to cry.

Pastor Jamal stood up to the podium to address the congregation with tears streaming down his face. "The Lord's spirit is here, let's not quench it. Let us go forward in dance."

Praise dancers came forth. Their garments were beautiful. The ladies were all in white attire with the men all dressed in white and blue. The flaggers moved across the altar holding flags with blue, white and gold in the fabric. Every time the dancers moved the flags Jenny could feel the wind going across the front. Several flaggers began to move back and forth with each aisle as the members moved up toward the front of the church.

Jenny was amazed at the beautiful garments the praise team had on. Some of the praise team was submerged in worship and couldn't go forth in dance. When they passed where Jenny sat the entire bench fell on their knees and began to cry to God. Jenny was caught up in the Spirit with the rest of the people who sat with her. She did not want the moment to end but before she knew it the service was over. Pastor Floyd was closing out.

After service, Jenny got up to leave and passed the pastor as he talked to someone else. Jamal reached out and grabbed Jenny's hand.

Pastor Jamal Floyd was speaking to Elder Fred and his wife. "I will handle that as soon as I can and get back to you Elder. You and your wife enjoy the rest of the day. I need to speak with Sister Jenkins for a moment."

Pastor Floyd stepped to his left to speak to Jenny. "Sister Jenny, excuse me, please." He moved past Elder Fred and his wife to motion to First Lady Joyce to come over. Joyce nodded. She made her way toward him and Jenny.

"Yes, Pastor." Jenny leaned in and kissed Joyce on the cheek. Joyce moved to give Jamal a hug. Jenny admired how Pastor Floyd loved his wife. She knew how genuine their relationship was because of their friendship. Jenny watched closely at the way Jamal treated Joyce the same outside of the church as he did inside. Jamal also showed the same respect and love toward his wife at all times.

Jamal always opened the door for Joyce when they were getting in and out of the car. The pastor helped his wife up and down the stairs. He was patient, unlike George, who walked ahead of Jenny and did not care if she stumbled. Jamal Floyd was not as tall as George but his love for his wife was ten feet taller than George.

"How are you? It's been an awhile since the last time we spoke. I know you keep in contact with First Lady Floyd, but I haven't spoken to you and brother George. I have called the both of you but never received a call back. I also left plenty of messages for brother George to call me. I just want to check on you two for myself. How are you doing?"

Jenny looked at the watch on her wrist and realized it's way past the time she needed to be home to prepare Sunday dinner. She prayed this doesn't take long. "Pastor, it is what it is. There's no need to talk about it. It's the same mess, nothing changes."

Jamal noticed Jenny being fidgety and knew it had something to do with her husband. He was concerned "and what mess is that sister Jenny?"

"Life, Pastor. God made mine hard for me. It seems like nothing is going right for me. My life is turning upside down and I don't think God even cares." Jenny stumbled a little and Jamal grabbed her before she hit the side of the pew.

"Here Sister Jenny, sit right here', Jamal stepped out of the way so she could sit down with Joyce's help. "You believe that Sister Jenny?"

Joyce softly touched Jenny on her back. She stared at Jenny and saw the tiredness. For the first time in weeks, Joyce noticed how much thinner Jenny had gotten. She wondered how much weight Jenny must have lost in the last month. Joyce grew weary at that moment.

"Yes Pastor, I do, I had my oldest son incarcerated for five years already. My twins, one who wants nothing to do with education. His sole goal is to be a womanizer. Then there's Paula, my only daughter. God only knows living out here reckless and doing whatever she wants to. I won't begin with their father. George doesn't love me, I know this. I can feel this. He doesn't touch me, nor does he spend any time with me. Shoot, he barely comes home any more unless it is time to eat. I believe he hates me...actually, I know he does." Jenny began to cry.

"Mother, your oldest child is locked up for the choices he made," Jamal stated his words very carefully. "God had nothing to do with that. Seek the Lord to uncover the source of perversion for your baby son. It's not God honey. It's the choices they made. God didn't deal you these cards, you chose to keep the hand that life dealt you, not God."

Jenny was stunned that Pastor Floyd would say such a thing to her. "That is so insensitive for you to say Pastor. I didn't choose to keep this hand; it was forced on me. I did not know I was playing cards. Who wants to suffer and live the life I'm living? Not me and not you. I didn't choose to live this way. Everyone else is not going through what I'm going through. God dealt a whole hard hand for me."

Jamal wasn't trying to be mean to her at all. "Jenny, you have it all wrong. God does not deal out cards for our life. God plans, but even during all that, He still allows us to make a choice. 'Choose this day whom you will serve.' We all have a choice.

You cannot blame God for the choices man made or makes. Your family has a choice as well."

"I hear you, Pastor. I feel different. My life has been hard all my life. These are the cards I feel like were given to me without my permission. I never had any choice in the matter." Jenny stood to leave and Joyce stood up beside her to make sure she didn't fall.

"Some people are facing struggles that will amaze you, and you do not know about them. Never compare your life to others. You have my number. Call me sometimes. Try to bring Johnny and Paula. It's been a long time since I saw them. I know the First Lady speaks to you more than I do but I would love to get more involved, especially with Johnny. Maybe there's something I can do with him. I truly believe I can help."

"I will, Pastor. I have to talk to George about it. You already know how he feels with me coming to church. I will discuss it with him and let First Lady Floyd know. Thank you."

Pastor Jamal Floyd hugged Jenny, "Do that Jenny. I'm always here if you ever need me and I think you do. Remember, I'm just a phone call away."

Chapter 5

Jenny was in the kitchen preparing Sunday dinner and setting the table. George sat at the table along with Paula. Both of them were texting at the same time. Neither saw Jenny almost drop the pot. She moved slowly and tried to get dinner on the table before George said anything. Jenny usually had everything ready by now. She looked around and noticed that Johnny was not there. Jenny pulled her hair back into a braid because the sweat was causing her hair to stick to the back of her neck.

"Has anyone seen John John?" Neither of the Jenkins at the table answered her. Both were on their cell phone texting and not paying her any attention at all.

"Paula? Did you hear what I asked? Please put down your phone while you are at the table." Jenny took Paula's phone out of her hand.

"What! What! Mommy I was texting Judy. Please, give me back my phone...please."

"Have you seen Johnny? And not while you are at the table, it's so rude. This is family time. Your friend can wait for you to finish eating."

"No, I haven't. Ask Daddy. Daddy has his phone at the table too!" Paula folded her arms across her chest and pouted. "I haven't seen Johnny."

George looked up at Jenny, "Do not ask me anything." He touched Paula's arm and said. "I pay all the bills including the phone you are currently on. I do not have to listen to your mother. Looking at Jenny, George aimed to prove a point, "Do I?"

"Never mind, I'll just put his plate in the oven." Jenny hated when George reminded them he paid all the bills. He forgot she did the paperwork for the Trucking Company and she helped build it from the ground and up.

"Are you about finished? I'm hungry." George finally looked up from his phone. "What's wrong with you? My food should have been hot and served by now!"

"I'm moving as fast as I can," Jenny snapped. The nonsense she knew was coming started to unfold. George was already simmering. He got worked up about her private meeting with Pastor Floyd after church. Jenny had told him because she didn't want him hearing it from anyone else. But, that didn't stop George from fussing the moment she came through the door.

Most Sundays, George would be asleep when she got home. Jenny would have to wake him. But today, George was wide awake and angry that she hadn't been there when he came back in. George had started earlier that morning and was still on his rampage.

"I only have two hands," Jenny said, her voice raised as she walked toward the table carrying the plates. "It would be nice if you or Paula helped me for a change."

"The food would've been ready if you hadn't been at church all day and then off having a private meeting with that hypocrite. What kind of man of the cloth shuts himself in a room with another man's wife, behind closed doors, like that? It's rude. It's disrespectful."

"Come on George, not today and not in front of Paula. It wasn't a private meeting. It was inside the church and First Lady Floyd was right there as well. Half the church was still there."

George glared at Jenny, fury in his eyes. "I'm just saying. If you weren't at church kissing up to that pastor's ass, my dinner would be on the table, hot and ready when I got home. Seems to me your god means more to you than I do. What's that scripture say? 'Wives, submit yourselves to your husbands'? You're not doing much of that, are you, Jenny?"

Jenny stumbled as she lost her footing. The plates clattered hard against the table. To anyone watching, it looked like she'd slammed them down on purpose. Truth was, part of her wished she had. Part of Jenny wished she could smash every last plate across George's head. George looked up from his phone just as the plates hit the table with a loud clatter.

"Oh, so now we're slamming plates?" he said, his voice sharp. "Did your God instruct you to do that? Would He approve of that attitude? Because from where I'm sitting, all that church mess isn't helping you much. You definitely have an attitude today, Mrs. Jenkins."

Jenny set Paula's plate on the table, then her own, and sank into the chair.

How would you know? You don't even go, Jenny thought even though she bit her tongue. She wouldn't dare say it to George and not today. Jenny didn't have the strength to argue with George.

"The food is ready, could one of you say grace?" Jenny says between clenched teeth.

George was irritated, "Didn't you pray enough while you were at church? You spent most of the day there. Why don't you pray, since you do it everyday. One more prayer won't matter.

Paula ate in silence while George talked, her jaw tight. He was one of the reasons she treated men the way she did.

After everything she had seen, the way George hurt her mother, and the pain they'd all lived through, Paula had lost every ounce of respect for her father. Men were all jerks in her eyes. George was the proof. Paula didn't trust any men. The teenage girl had made up her mind a long time ago: she would do men in before they ever got the chance to do her in.

Jenny turned to her daughter as a last resort, "Paula?"

"Mommy, I don't feel like praying. God won't hear my prayers." Paula looked over at her dad. "He won't hear Daddy's prayers either."

George looked at Paula still fuming, "It all depends what god you are praying to. If it's your mother's god, he probably won't. He doesn't like me."

Paula burst out laughing. She knew that her father was joking but she knew it was true.

Jenny began to pray, "Lord, we bless this food in Jesus' name. Amen."

Jenny shook her head at the both of them and continued the prayer. "And Lord watch over Johnny because he knows he should be in this house for dinner."

George clapped his hands, "Nice and short! That's how I like it...nice and short." He grabbed a roll from the basket in the middle of the table with a chuckle.

The patio door swung open and Johnny came in with his friend Kent right behind him.

"Hey, Mom," Johnny said. He leaned down to kiss Jenny on the cheek before he rubbed his father's head on the way past.

Kent grinned, reached over, and ruffled Paula's hair.

"Boy, don't touch me!" Paula swatted Kent's hand away. She scowled, while the boys laughed and stepped back.

Kent and Johnny had been best friends since fifth grade. They played football together for years, until Kent quit to help at home when his mom was diagnosed with cancer. When

Johnny mentioned Sunday dinner, Kent jumped at the chance to come along. Kent's mom usually worked Sundays. Most nights, the young boy survived on pizza, fast food, or whatever his mom brought home from the restaurant.

Johnny reached over and tugged one of George's dreads. George smacked him lightly on the back of his head. "Boy, you trying to size me up?"

"Hold on, Pops!" Johnny said laughing. "I'm not trying to size you up, I just like your cut."

George rubbed his own head and chuckled. "Oh, that's what you were doing? I thought you were trying to size me up. Nice, right? I keep trying to tell you, my barber's the truth."

Johnny shook his head and said, "I'm good, Pop. I'm trying to grow my hair out. I need a new look for the ladies. Mom, where is my plate, I'm starving?"

Kent grinned, hopeful. "Mrs. Jenkins...mine too?"

Jenny looked up from her plate, surprised but smiling. "In the oven. I wasn't expecting you, Kent. But, I'll fix you a plate." Kent happily took a seat at the table.

"Thank you Mrs. Jenkins," he said with a sigh of relief. Kent loved Jenny's cooking. Next to his grandmother, she was the best cook ever.

Johnny got his plate out of the oven while Jenny got up to make Kent's plate. Jenny pointed toward the sink.

"Go wash your hands, young men. And don't you dare touch my bread with those dirty fingers. Up! The both of you. You know better."

They both go to wash their hands. They playfully ran to see who could be there first and back to the table.

"Pop, I need fifty dollars. I asked Mom, but she said she doesn't have it." Johnny flashed a mischievous smile at his father. He slid onto the seat beside George and wrapped him in a hug.

George smirked, already knowing what was coming. Jenny had told him earlier, but he decided to play along anyway. George raised an eyebrow.

"For what?" he asked. "And do you even deserve fifty dollars? You didn't clean the backyard or cut the grass like I told you to."

Johnny grabbed his fork, ready to dive into his plate. "A fitted," he said, shaking his head. "And why would I do that when we have a gardener? That's their job. They get paid to do it."

George gave Johnny a puzzled look.

"Didn't I just give you two hundred dollars the other day?" he asked. "Maybe you should try doing some work around here for once. All your mama does is spoil you."

Johnny grinned.

"Come on, Pop because you already know what's up. I took the 200 you gave me and bought these." Johnny stuck his foot out, showing off the fresh sneakers. Then, he looked up at his dad with a proud smile.

George shook his head. "Yeah. I'm not giving it to you. That's the deal."

He wasn't falling for Johnny's shenanigans today. "Do some work around here," George added.

"It's about time you get a job and start paying your way. You're getting entitled, and money doesn't grow on trees or out of my pocket."

Paula stuck out her tongue at Johnny and laughed. Then she turned to her father, her eyes wide and playful like a puppy.

"Daddy..." she asked sweetly.

Paula buttering up to her father, "Daddy, could you give me a hundred dollars?"

Without hesitation, George pulled out his wallet. "Yeah, baby girl," he said, reaching inside and handing Paula a crisp hundred-dollar bill.

He nodded at Johnny, who immediately bristled.

Johnny smacked the money out of Paula's hand. "Hey, hey! How are you gonna give her a hundred? I only asked for fifty! That's not fair!" He shoved his plate away, glaring.

Paula always got her way with their father. Johnny hated the open favoritism George showed to Paula. He eyed her outfit, shaking his head. She'd changed again. Gone was the purple halter and booty shorts. Now, Paula sat there in a Little House on the Prairie sundress like butter wouldn't melt in her mouth. But Johnny didn't care. He was about to spill the tea on her.

Let's see how she handles this next move. Johnny thought to himself with resentment.

Paula jumped up and wrapped her arms around George. "I'm Daddy's favorite, right, Daddy?" she said with a grin.

Paula shot Johnny a look over her shoulder, smiling smugly before rolling her eyes at him. Paula always seemed to have a spell on George. She could get whatever she wanted from him. Truth be told, she had a way of getting what she wanted from anyone, men and women alike. People just seemed to fall under her charm. George hugged her back, his chest tightening. She looked so much like the younger Jenny he'd fallen in love with all those years ago.

"You're the prettiest," he said softly.

Paula's smile lit up the room like the evening star, drawing everyone's attention without her even trying. Her long, chocolate-brown hair was pulled into a tight braid, the fine coppery strands catching the light. George studied her, his heart heavy. She resembled Jenny so much; the smile, the confidence, the way she carried herself. It broke him a little inside knowing she was no longer a little girl, no longer innocent.

Her perfect white teeth flashed as she laughed, and George thought of how much money he'd spent to get them fixed. Pecan-skinned and headstrong, Paula took pride in her appearance just like her mother always had.

George's gaze drifted to Jenny. He shook his head and sighed. *I miss that Jenny,* he thought. He missed the one who had been so sure of herself.

Johnny flashed a sly smile at Paula. "And let's not forget: dumb, stupid, and ugly," he teased.

He stood and moved to sit beside her, his grin widening. Johnny was about to drop a bombshell. He knew how protective their father was over Paula. Johnny also knew that what he was about to say would hit hard. Jenny waved her hands at him.

"John John, watch your mouth and apologize to your sister," she scolded.

She hated when the twins went at each other like this, especially when George sat back and let it happen. Still, she couldn't deny Johnny was right about one thing; George spoiled Paula more than he should. Johnny's grin turned into a challenge as he looked straight at his dad.

"No! She always gets her way. Pop, did your baby girl tell you she didn't come into the house until this morning? Did your diamond tell you that?"

He turned to face Paula, locking eyes with her. Paula's spoon slipped from her fingers and clattered against the plate.

"Checkmate," Johnny said with a smirk. George's head snapped up from his plate.

"Paula?" His voice was calm but firm. "What is he talking about? Did you come into this house this morning? What time did you get home?" Paula coughed and forced a smile.

"Stop lying, Johnny. You're always lying. You're just mad because Daddy gave me money."

George's voice hardened. Paula knew she was in trouble. So, she did what she always did to get out of the heat. Paula tried to make Johnny look like the liar.

"Daddy, you can't believe anything John John says. He's lying."

Johnny smirked. He'd been waiting for that. "I knew you'd say that." He pulled out his phone and held it up.

"I'm lying? Really? Watch this." Paula lunged across the table, trying to grab the phone, but Johnny jumped back, laughing. He leaned over toward George, holding the screen where his father could see.

"I record everything, don't I, Daddy?"

George coughed, his spoon slipping from his hand and clattering onto the table. Jenny shook her head slowly, disappointment heavy in her expression. She didn't need to see the video to know Johnny wasn't lying. Now she waited for George to react. The room went silent. Everyone's eyes were on George and Paula, waiting for him to explode. Instead, George reached into his pocket, pulled out another hundred-dollar bill, and handed it to Johnny.

"You're grounded," George said flatly, looking at Paula. "I told you about coming into this house late at night."

Paula's mouth fell open. What no one else at the table knew was that George's anger was mixed with something else…fear. George hated the fact that Johnny knew he was still cheating on Jenny. One afternoon, Johnny saw his father parked outside the mall, but he wasn't alone. Cassandra sat beside him in the car as she laughed and leaned a little too close. Suspicious, Johnny snapped a quick picture and texted George, "Who's the lady you with, Dad?"

Startled, George jumped in his seat, his phone buzzing with Johnny's message. He quickly tried to come up with a lie. He was ready to say Cassandra was there to meet Rick. But before he could even respond, Cassandra leaned over and kissed him full on the mouth. That moment sealed it. Johnny had caught everything.

From that day forward, George's own son held the secret over his head. Johnny used what he knew to blackmail his father. George hated that his son had power over him. The prideful man resented that he couldn't risk a divorce when most of what he owned was in Jenny's name, even half of the trucking business. Still, as much as he despised it, part of George was proud. Johnny stood his ground. George respected Johnny's threats, even if he had to pay the price.

"Answer me, young lady. What time did you come in this house?" George's voice was low and hard.

"You keep playing with me, Paula. You're going to get somebody hurt, or worse. You're not grown. You're not a woman yet. Who were you out with until morning?" He shook his head before she could answer.

"Never mind. You'd just lie anyway." Feeling both defeated and full, George pushed back from the table, stood, and left the room without another word. Johnny leaned closer to Paula, his voice a taunt.

"I guess you're grounded, Diamond. And remember, I'm watching you too." Johnny smirked.

"You're just like Dad in more ways than you think. Like father, like daughter. I'm always watching you."

Paula shot him a furious look, then bolted from the table and ran to her room in tears. Jenny sighed and followed after her. Johnny burst out laughing. Kent didn't even pause. He kept eating, glancing around like he was watching one of his mom's soap operas. He shook his head.

"Wow, man. You something else," he said, reaching for another roll. "I'm gonna pray for y'all. I'm going to make sure I start with you."

Johnny grabbed another piece of chicken and grinned. "I know," he said, still laughing.

The two friends finished their plates in silence, not saying another word. The walls of this house held more than laughter and love. They held secrets, whispered in the dark and tucked away behind closed doors. In a family where loyalty was twisted and truth was bought with dollar bills, the cracks in the foundation grew wider with every lie told and every truth left unspoken.

Chapter 6

Paula stretched out on the couch in the family room, a book open in her hands. She wasn't reading, not really. She was still fuming at Johnny for snitching on her. That's what he did best.

Even though they were twins, Paula and Johnny were nothing alike. Johnny was too soft. Paula was tougher. But she had to admit, he'd stepped up his game this time. She would have to be more careful next time.

The doorbell rang suddenly. The sound was startling, loud and urgent, like someone was after them. Paula groaned. Ever since her dad made her mom get rid of the maid, every knock or ring meant she had to get up and answer it herself. The bell rang again, followed by a heavy knock that sounded like the police pounding on the door. Too lazy to get up at first, she called toward the door.

"Who is it?"

"It's Rick. Let me in."

Paula's heart skipped. Of course it was Rick. He already knew she was home. George had told him what happened last night, and told him she was grounded. Rick had been calling her all night, but she hadn't answered. This morning, he'd even called from a burner phone so her parents wouldn't see his number. Paula finally got up and opened the door. Rick rushed past her into the house. He moved quickly, checking the hallway and peeking toward the bedrooms to make sure her parents weren't around. Rick looked nervous, running a hand over his forehead before turning back to Paula.

She stood there in his favorite white sundress, a small, knowing smile playing at her lips. She hadn't needed to talk to him to know he would come.

Paula wasn't in the mood for Rick's attitude. She already knew he was worked up. He always got like this when he couldn't reach her.

"What's wrong with you?" she snapped.

Rick rushed toward her, his face tense. "Where were you last night? Why didn't you answer my calls?"

He grabbed her by the shoulders, his grip too tight. Paula shoved him back.

"Johnny got me in trouble, that's what happened! Daddy took my phone, so I had no way to call you back. I was here all night."

Rick's eyes darted to the coffee table. He snatched up Paula's phone and turned to her. "So what's this? This is your phone, right? Why are you lying to me?"

Paula ripped it out of his hand. "I'm not lying! Daddy did take my phone. He just gave it back to me this morning before they left."

Rick ran a hand down his face, frustration written all over him. "I thought your dad took it. How do you have it now?"

He knew he sounded crazy, but this is what Paula did to him. Every time she missed his calls, he ended up here, desperate for answers. Paula rolled her eyes and let out a sharp sigh.

"You are bugging. You need to chill, sir."

Rick shook his head. "Why are you always lying to me, Paula? I've got to end this before we get caught. I can't keep doing this. You're like a niece to me. This is all wrong."

He sank onto the couch, burying his face in his hands.

"This is wrong," he muttered. "I've got to stop this. I feel like a pervert and a child molester."

Paula slid closer to him on the couch, her voice low and coaxing. "But it doesn't feel wrong," she whispered.

She touched his arm gently and her expression softened. Paula couldn't afford to lose him, not now. She had plans, and Rick was a big part of them. Rick's eyes darted toward the window, his nerves showing.

"Where are your parents? Did they leave yet?" Paula smiled, leaning back against the couch.

"They drove the snitch to Grandmamma Alice's house. You know that's a long drive."

She folded her arms, watching him carefully, knowing she had him right where she wanted him. Rick's grip tightened slightly as he pulled Paula closer.

"What time did they leave?" he asked, his voice low.

Every part of him screamed to stop, to walk away, but Paula had a hold on him that he couldn't explain. She was intoxicating, like a witch casting a spell he couldn't break. She was young, only sixteen and half, but she carried herself with a confidence that pulled him in every time. And no matter how many times he told himself it was wrong, Rick's body betrayed him. He couldn't help himself. Paula smiled knowingly and brushed her hand down his chest. She had him, and she knew it.

Paula moved closer to Rick.

"An hour ago, more like 45 minutes, I talked to Daddy already."

Rick began to calculate the time, 'That's about a three-hour trip one way and three hours coming back. Rick moved closer to Paula. He started to unbutton her dress and he realized she had no panties on when he touched her thigh.

"Yes, they're gone the whole day. Alone at home with no school is something I love." She lifted her dress up.

Rick kissed her inner leg, "Me too. Let's go to my place."

He was scared they may get caught. Rick felt safer at his place. Most of his neighbors thought Paula was his niece and she hung over his house like most nieces do.

"No, I have to stay here because Mommy calls me. She calls me every 15 minutes."

Rick began to unbuckle his pants belt to take off his pants. "Why didn't you go to Momma Alice's house?"

"I lied and told them I had to work today. I haven't told them I am not working anymore yet."

"When are you going to tell your parents you are not working anymore?" Pulling his pants down so he can step out of them.

"When you stop paying me. It's pay day in body and cash." Paula pulled her dress over her head. Rick smiled and slapped her on her buttocks.

"Girl, you turn me on inside and out. I have to end this. I can't keep doing this. It's all wrong. Paula, you are young enough to be my child."

Paula licked Rick's neck, "But I'm not your daughter. Are you sure you want to end this? Touching him where it mattered the most, Paula took off her bra and her breast popped out.

Rick buries his face in her large breast, "My God, they sit like pears and they are so huge." He began to cry. Rick wanted this to end but couldn't help himself. He took one of her nipples into his mouth.

Paula pushed him off her and threw her dress at him. She pushed him onto the couch and grabbed his face. Paula positions herself over Rick.

"Candy misses you, Papi?"

Rick cried out to her, "My God, you Jezebel, I can't take this."

"But you want to. I miss you. My kitty misses you. Don't you miss her Papi?

"This is all wrong."

Paula moved down and positioned Rick inside of her and let out a loud sigh. Rick grabbed Paula around her waist.

Paula knew she had him where she wanted him."But you feel so good on the inside."

When Rick got like this Paula knew he would last longer without the blue pills. Paula made sure Rick was harder than ever because she was stressed. She needed every bit of what Rick was offering her.

"Yes, yes it does." Rick thrust forward and the tears began to run down his cheeks.

"This is all wrong." Rick covered his face in her breast.

"Are you sure you want to end this?" Paula pulled away from him, Rick pulled her back.

"Not today," Rick lifted her up and carried her to her bedroom. Paula laughed in victory. She wanted him more than he wanted her right now. Steve had a game and he wasn't putting out. Rick would have to satisfy her.

"Kitty is happy now. Give her some of your lollipop."

"I'm going to give you all this lollipop." he threw Paula on her bed. She burst out laughing.

Rick forgot about breaking it off with Paula. He would do it later, he promised.

Chapter 7

Jenny and George's bedroom was a comfortable place to rest and sleep as long as George was not at home. The large elegant pendant lights provided a warm glow in the evening setting an atmosphere for prayer. A two-tone wall design had a smoky grey paint color on the lower portion, while a crisp white upper portion drew the eyes to the light fixtures hanging from the ceiling. To bring the two together, a centrally positioned floral painting featured both of the colors, as well as the dusty white tones from the bedding. Jenny loved their bedroom; it was a place of escape from the day to day troubles she had been facing within her family lately.

For the past hour or so Jenny had been on her knees attempting to pray. She was determined to get this prayer out but she seemed distracted a little bit. Jenny got her Bible and randomly opened it to any chapter.

"What's wrong with me, why can't I pray? Lord, I need a word," she sat there with her Bible open and then prayed out to the Lord.

"Lord, please help me. I desire to hear from you. I desire to pray. What's wrong with me? I'm trying to pray, but I can't." Jenny picked up the Bible again.

"Oh please," she went into the kitchen and turned on the radio. Jenny sat on the couch rocking to the music. She became frustrated because she didn't understand what was going on. Jenny got up and began to pace the floor.

"Lord, what's wrong with me? I used to love being in your presence. What's happened? Why can't I just push Lord? I feel like I'm dying; I feel so dried up. Help me, Jesus. Help me Holy Spirit to get back to you!"

As Jenny prayed, the phone rang. At first, she wasn't going to answer. It was another distraction. The answering machine came on and Jenny heard her a familiar sound. GT was calling from prison.

"This is a collect call from Delmont Corrections Center, to accept the call press 1. Press 2 to reject and hang up." Jenny gave up on praying and picked up the phone. She pressed 1 and sighed already knowing what GT was calling about. GT was nearly done serving time for his last mess up.

"Hello, George."

"Mom, I asked you to call me GT, please. Do not call me George. I am a grown man. I have outgrown that name."

"Hey GT, what's going on?" Jenny laid down on the couch and pulled out one of the throw covers. She was a bit too cold.

"Mom, I'm calling to make sure you and dad are going to be here to pick me up. You know it's only a few days before I come home. I'm just checking with you guys to make sure y'all haven't forgotten."

"Who else is coming, GT? Do you have someone else who is picking you up? This is your fifth time this week calling about who is going to pick you up. You know I'll be there to get you. Me and your father will be there to get you."

"I don't know, Mom. I haven't seen or heard from you lately. You hardly ever pick up when I call, which makes me question and worry that I might not be your first priority. I haven't seen you in the 5 years since I've been here. Daddy answers my calls all the time. You don't. So, yes I have to ask because it seems you forgot about me."

GT was Jenny and George's oldest child. He was 21 years old and had been locked up for five years. Jenny got pregnant with him when she was just 17 years old. She was a senior in high school. It was a struggle because she was living in an abusive household. Jenny had been running the streets with George since she was 16 to escape. Jenny originally planned to have an abortion because she wanted to attend college, but George refused to let her kill their unborn child. Instead Jenny moved in with George.

GT was named after his father and grandfather; George Terrance Jenkins III. GT hated his name. The young man had been in and out of group homes since he was younger. He was such a good kid but one day he woke up completely different. He became so angry and violent overnight. No matter what Jenny and George tried to do to help him, GT just became angrier. His anger landed him in prison.

One day GT was robbed for his drug stash by three men. The men jumped and beat him violently. As they were walking away with his drugs, GT grabbed a gun and shot all three repeatedly. One boy died from his injuries. One was left blind and paralyzed. The other hadn't been the same ever since. The prosecutor argued it wasn't self defense because the boys were walking away.

GT was facing capital murder along with 2 counts of attempted murder and three counts of assault with a deadly weapon. Jenny fasted day in and day out for her son. She took money out of the savings her grandfather left her to get GT the best lawyer around. Somehow, the young boy only got five years in prison with three years served while his case was in court. He only had to do two years because evidence came out that the same boys who robbed GT had just robbed and murdered an older woman and her husband.

Even though her son thought it was a time to celebrate, Jenny was upset with GT. She told GT about a dream she had and warned him something was going to happen. She told him to stop selling drugs. The day he was found not guilty on the murder and attempted murder charges, Jenny told GT she was done. Jenny told him she wasn't coming to see GT while he was locked up. She kept every word. GT was upset with his mother because he hadn't seen her in two years. His dad and John John had come. GT's grandma, Juanita, has been several times as well. But, Jenny and Paula did not make one visit.

"I told you GT, if you go to prison again, I was not coming to see you like I did the last six times. Besides, a lot has been going on."

"Tell me something new. Every time I speak to you something is always going on besides a visit, a letter or putting money on my books. That's the only thing that has not been going on with you since I've been here."

"Excuse me! Say that again, so I can be sure I heard you correctly."

GT cleared his voice trying not to disrespect his mother. He responded a little calmer. "I'm just saying, every time I turn around, something is going on. You don't come visit; you don't send money. I barely hear from you guys. I feel lonely up here, Mom. I feel like my family has abandoned me. Do you know how it feels to hear other inmates' names called for a visit and my name is only called once or twice a month and never from my mother?"

Jenny defensively responded to GT, "I don't like your tone. I told you if you get locked up again I wasn't coming. I meant every word of that. I've been running in and out of the prison system with you for years. How much longer did you think I'm going to keep putting up with you being locked up?"

"Whatever mom. It doesn't surprise me, it's been like this all my life. If you felt this way why fight for me. Why? They robbed me and beat me. I did nothing wrong. But do you even care that I was innocent this time."

It was not easy expressing his feelings to his mother. Jenny took everything GT said as an attack. It had been like that for years. This day was no different. Jenny and GT always wound up arguing. GT loved his mother. He had to admit he has caused a lot of the friction between them. If Jenny only knew what GT's secrets were maybe, just maybe, she would give him a pass for his anger.

"IF you weren't selling drugs or had listened to me...IF you were in the house like I told you to be, you wouldn't have gotten robbed. This would have never happened. You are there for being hard-headed and not listening to me. Do not get upset with me when I told you over and over again that I was not coming to visit you."

Jenny got colder and shivered even though she was under the throw. She cleared her throat and bowed out of the argument with her son. "Do you need anything else, GT?"

"Yeah, where is Paula? I need to talk to her. She's not responding to me. I really need to talk to her.

"She's not here. What is going on between you two? You guys ain't never been this way with each other. You guys were so close. Now you act like you hate each other. I don't get what's going on between you two."

"Nothing mom, nothing, I do not hate my sister. She hates me. I really need to talk to her. I will talk to you later. Just promise me you'll be here to pick me up next week."

"I promise GT, You keep saying nothing's going on between you and Paula but I don't like this tension between you two. I'll be there. We will be there to get you GT, don't worry about it."

"Ok mom, I really do love you. Please let Paula know I've been trying to get in contact with her. It's very important that I talk to her."

"The jail recorder came on to let them know time was about up for the call. Jenny calls out to her son, "GT, hold on!"

"Yeah?"

"I apologize for everything I did. I apologize for everything I allowed in your life. I love you, GT. I really do wish I could change a lot of things but I can't. I pray when you get out we can begin to heal and things will be better between us. I pray things are better between you and your sister too. I love you son. Never forget that."

GT felt a little frustrated and spat back at the apology, "Action speaks louder than words. Talk to you later, mom."

"I love you, GT! Please don't forget that."

GT hung up just as Paula, Kent and Johnny came in the door. Johnny kissed his mother on the cheeks. "Was that big bro? Man, I missed his call! I should have come in the house earlier.

Jenny pulled back from Johnny, giving him and Kent a side look. "How was school today?"

"School was fine," Johnny and Kent laughed thinking about the school fight that broke out during lunch the day before.

"Really? What did you learn today?"

Kent spoke up first, "Math, English, Reading and Gym."

"I didn't ask you to name your classes. I asked what you learned."

"Come on, Mom. We learned a lot today. It's too much to remember off the top of my head. I have to think about it. You know, since the teacher barely knows even knows what they're talking about."

Jenny hated that she listened to Johnny when he asked her to go to Princeton Elite school, a school for the gifted and smart. Most of the time Johnny didn't listen or go to class because he was bored. It wasn't his grades that were the problem. Johnny kept ditching class.

Jenny continued to press the boy, "What did you learn? I'm going to ask you one last time, Johnny."

"What we didn't do yesterday. We learned that." Johnny laughed, punching Kent in his arm.

Jenny knew neither Johnny or Kent were in school because the principal called her. Jenny asked John John one last time knowing he would lie. "And what was that?"

"Nothing," Johnny and Kent blurted out as they both laughed.

Johnny hadn't attended school. He hung out at Kent's house helping him babysit his little sister. The usual babysitter called right before they were leaving for school to tell Kent's mom that she couldn't come due to a family emergency. Kent's mother couldn't afford to call out so Kent told her he would stay home. Johnny said he would stay with him since he wasn't going to school anyway. Johnny got in trouble several times correcting his math teacher. The teacher felt Johnny was being disrespectful for correcting him in front of the other students. They had a test tomorrow and Johnny would ace it without studying for it.

"I'll be coming to your school tomorrow to ask all your teachers about *nothing*. Paula, GT just called asking for you! He said he's been calling you, but you refuse all his phone calls. Why?"

Paula rolled her eyes. She did not like her brother. When they were growing up, all Jenny and George ever did was focus on GT more than her and Johnny. GT had always been their golden child.

"I don't know why he is asking for me. I have nothing to say to him. He should know this by now."

"I don't get it. You and GT used to be so close. Now, you act like you hate your own brother."

Paula rolled her eyes once again and sucked her teeth. "We were never close. I was just young, and I didn't know any better."

Johnny shook his head at Paula. "That makes little sense. You didn't know any better. That's your brother. You're supposed to love your brother, stupid."

"Shut up! Nobody is talking to you. They never do."

Jenny butt in before an argument exploded. "What's going on between you and GT Paula? He won't tell me and you won't tell me."

Paula dodged the conversation about GT, "I don't want to talk about it, I'm meeting up with Judy at the mall. Remember, mommy? I asked you if I could go."

"Don't be too late getting back in here Paula you know tonight is a school night. You already know how your father is about you coming in here late."

Paula nodded as she left the house. Johnny turned to his mother, "That's your daughter, your demon child.

Chapter 8

George sat on the back patio, a cold mug of beer in his hand. "This is something I haven't done in a long time," he muttered to himself, taking a slow sip. The morning was quiet. He glanced toward the pool house, admiring the work he'd recently done there. For a moment, he let himself relax. Jenny and the twins were out running errands.

Finally, the busy man had a little peace, but George's mind wouldn't let him rest. Last night's encounter with Cassandra drained him. The weight of the affair clung to George's skin like the scent of cheap perfume and regret. Every word she whispered replayed in his mind, twisting between guilt and desire. George told himself it would be the last time he came home. He claimed to be done with Jenny, but deep down, George knew he was lying to himself.

What started as an escape had become a trap that slowly pulled him further away from everything that once mattered. Trying to run a successful trucking company while balancing two households was taking its toll. Something had to give.

George needed to talk to someone…someone other than Rick. He'd called his mother earlier, but she hadn't been available. Now, as his phone buzzed, he saw her name on the screen. She was calling him back. He exhaled slowly before answering.

"Hi, Mother. Thanks for returning my call."

Juanita's voice was warm but sharp with concern. "Hey, son. How are you? You never call me this early."

George hesitated. "I'm…not doing too good today," he admitted. "I need to talk to you about something."

Juanita's concern deepened.

"What's wrong? Are you sick? Is the business in trouble?"

"No, nothing like that. I'm just…tired. Worn out. I'm not feeling sick. It's something else."

"What is it? What's wrong with you?" Juanita pressed. "Maybe you need to see a doctor. Do you want me to come over?"

"No," George said quickly. "There's no need to come over, Mom. Just…listen, okay? I need to get this off my chest. Can I be honest with you?"

"Yes, you can," she said softly. "Go ahead. I'm listening."

George stared out over the yard, his chest tight. He didn't know how his mother was going to take what he was about to say. Juanita loved Jenny; everyone knew that. She had always supported Jenny, sometimes siding with her over him. George felt like Juanita was punishing him and his brother for the things their father had done. But he couldn't hold it in any longer.

"Mom…" He took a deep breath. "I want a divorce." He froze. He couldn't believe he'd actually said it out loud.

On the other end of the line, Juanita fell silent. She stared at the phone in her hand, almost as if she'd misheard him.

"From who?" she said finally, her voice quiet but firm. George winced.

"From Jenny. You heard me the first time," he said, already regretting saying it out loud. "I know you're upset. Maybe I should've kept it to myself. But you know what me and Jenny have gone through before, Mom. You already know I'm not happy in this marriage. And I know what you're about to say."

"Jenny who?" Juanita asked sharply. "And yes. You should know. Because we've all been through this before. Not just you and Jenny, the whole family. So I'll ask again, George…Jenny who?"

George swallowed hard. "My wife. The mother of my kids, Jenny." He gripped the phone tighter.

"Mom, it's different this time. I just need you to listen. I've thought about this for a while now—"

"God help us," Juanita cut into her son's words, her voice rising. "You don't need a divorce from your wife. There must be another name. Some other woman. You can't be talking about the Jenny. Not the mother of my grandbabies. Not the woman who worked herself half to death so you could finish school, who supported you through everything. The one who went through difficult twin pregnancies while she worked and nearly drove herself into the grave just to keep you afloat!"

Juanita's tone sharpened even more, anger breaking through her hurt.

"You cannot be talking about my daughter-in-law. The one who is sweet and kind and puts up with all the mess you've been putting her through. Who is she, George? What's her name? And don't you dare tell me it's that same old whore from before. It better not be her."

George closed his eyes. He knew exactly who his mother meant: Cassandra. Juanita started again, her voice trembled with anger.

"George, do you even know who this woman is? Do you know the kind of person you're letting into your life, or worse, into your marriage?"

"Why do you believe there's another woman?" George asked, frustration creeping into his voice.

"You're always thinking the worst of me. I'm not Daddy."

Juanita's reply was sharp, but her voice cracked with hurt. "Any man who cheats on his wife asks that same question. You're acting just like your father. And then you get mad when I say it. George, I never wanted you to turn out like him. But it's breaking my heart to see you mistreat your beautiful wife like this. Jenny is a good woman. She is a woman you have run over for years. I pray you don't end up like your father."

George's grip tightened on the phone. "Mom, you're not making any sense. I'm nothing like my father."

"Daddy died full of secrets and shame," George snapped.

Juanita's voice sharpened. She responded steadily but wounded, "No, you're the one not making sense."

"He had everything most men dream of: wealth, influence, and a future already mapped out...and still, he carried a secret that ate him alive. Shame came from what he hid. You are going down the same path," she fired back.

"Why can't it just be that I'm not happy anymore?" George asked, his voice rising. "Why can't it just be that I'm tired? I am not my father, and I need you to stop saying that."

Juanita didn't back down. "You weren't tired when Jenny was helping you get your GED and paying for college. You weren't unhappy when she was pregnant with twins and working two full-time jobs to keep the lights on.

"This is the wife who took her inheritance and helped you build your company from the ground up. The wife you've cheated on more than once without any reason to.

"So tell me, George. How are you not your father when you keep repeating every single mistake he made? You want an award because you haven't laid hands on her? That's the only difference you can claim."

George swallowed hard, regret gnawed at him. He wasn't angry at what his mother was said. George was angry because every word was true. He hated being compared to his father. His father had been a cruel man, and George had sworn he would never be like him.

"Mom—"

"George," Juanita cut him off. "I covered for you last time you cheated. God knows it my heart, because I love Jenny like a daughter. But you can't fool me this time.

"I know you, George. All the signs are there. And I pray to God it's not the same Jezebel as before. We barely dodged a bullet last time. Please tell me it's not her."

Juanita's voice dropped, almost a whisper now. "I know it is. I know it's her. That woman has her claws in you, George. She's going to take you down a rabbit hole, and you're going to lose your entire family over her."

George said nothing.

And in his silence, Juanita had her answer.

"George, I love you," Juanita said, her voice breaking. "But I cannot stand by you this time. I prayed you would've learned from what your father did to me. That man is dead and gone, and I'm still living with the consequences.

"I have HIV because your father didn't know how to stay faithful. Jenny is an excellent wife, George. I just pray to God you don't realize that too late."

George closed his eyes. "Mom, I love you. I feel how I feel. And that's not going to change."

Juanita let out a long, weary sigh. "I love you too, son. But I'm praying you get yourself together before you make a fool of yourself and before you make a decision you can't take back."

George's jaw tightened. "Pray to who?" he snapped.

Juanita went quiet for a moment. "Don't go there, George. Pray to your Heavenly Father. You know who I'm talking about."

George let out a bitter laugh, "Who...Daddy?"

"Yes your heavenly Father." Juanita said firmly, "Some people call Him Daddy. Some people call him Father. Some call Him God"

"But tell me, Mom. Do some people call Him George?" His voice hardened. "Because that's the only father I've known. And from what I know about him, he didn't make it to your so-called heaven."

"George." Juanita's tone sharpened. "I can say what I want about your father, but you stay respectful. No matter what your father did or didn't do, he was still your daddy. And I will not have you disrespect him."

George's chest ached. He ran a hand over his face, suddenly regretting this whole conversation. "This was a mistake," he muttered. "I shouldn't have said anything to you. Every time I try to tell you how I feel about me and Jenny, you go on the defense like I'm attacking you.

"You say I need to get myself together? Fine. But I feel the same way about you, Mom. Stop attacking me for what George Sr. did to you.

"I am not him. The problem is, you don't know that."

"George, George, George! Listen to me."

But George didn't want to hear another word. His chest burned with anger, guilt, and shame.

He pulled the phone from his ear and hung up on his mother.

The patio fell silent, except for the faint hum of the pool pump and the clink of his beer mug against the table.

Chapter 9

Jenny had been awake for over two hours. It was hard to focus, harder still to pray, with George lying next to her. George hadn't come home in weeks, but tonight he had. Instead of their usual tension, George took a shower and slipped into bed. For the first time in months, he reached for her. He held her close.

And then, quietly, almost tenderly, George made love to Jenny. Now he slept soundly. George breathed even, his body warm against hers. Jenny didn't dare move. For the first time in so long, George turned to her in his sleep, pulling her closer. It felt so good to be in his arms again. She thought about slipping out to the living room to pray, but no. Not tonight. Not when she had this rare moment of closeness.

So she stayed, lying still in the darkness, silently waiting for God to speak. And then, she heard Him.

Jenny. The Lord's voice was soft but unmistakable. Jenny's breath caught. She shifted slightly, careful not to wake George.

"Jenny."

Her heart pounded as she heard God call her name again. She moved a little more, trembling now, afraid of waking her husband but unable to stay still.

"Jenny, my daughter. I love you."

Jenny's tears slipped down her face before she could stop them. She whispered into the darkness, "I love you too."

"I know the thoughts I have toward you, Jenny. I will never leave you nor forsake you. I hear your cries. I am near to you."

Jenny slowly slid out of George's arms. Her recent weight loss made it easier. She knelt beside the bed, hands clasped tightly, her heart racing.

Why tonight? she wondered. *Why speak to me tonight of all nights, when George finally came home?*

"I love you, Lord," she whispered. "I miss you. I used to worship all the time. I used to pray every day. What's wrong with me?"

She kept her voice soft, careful not to disturb George.

"I am doing a new thing in you," the Lord said. I am taking you to the next dimension in worship. There is a reason I have you in this place. I need you to trust me. Can you trust me, Jenny?"

Jenny's shoulders shook as she whispered back, "Yes, Lord. I can trust You. But, it's been so hard. I don't understand why you've been so quiet. Why you've felt so far away. Why can't I feel you?"

George stirred and turned over. Jenny cracked one eye open, holding her breath until she was sure he was still asleep. Then she heard Him again.

"Sometimes I have to step back...so you can see you." Jenny frowned, confused by His words. Her whisper grew louder before she realized it. "I don't understand..."

"Sometimes I step back," the Lord said gently.

"Not to leave you, but so you can see what you are becoming. If I haven't told you that something is wrong, why do you keep believing it is? Why do you keep questioning who you are?"

Jenny wiped her tears. "Because I'm not praying or worshipping like I used to. I feel like I'm doing something wrong. And when I look at my life, everything feels like it's falling apart."

"Exactly," the Lord replied. *You keep saying, 'like I used to.' Jenny, I'm doing a new thing in you. It's time to move out of your comfort zone into something deeper. How else would you learn to chase after Me without trials? How else would you see Me as your strength?"

Jenny pressed her forehead against the mattress, weeping softly.

"I'm here, Jenny. I have not left you. I am always by your side."

"I love you, Father," Jenny whispered through her tears. "Oh my...this means the world to me. I've been waiting for this for so long."

Her voice grew louder as she cried. She didn't notice George stirring on the other side of her. George sat up in bed, his face dark with frustration.

George had come home after the difficult conversation with his mother, hoping that maybe there was still something left to salvage between him and Jenny. He'd even made love to her, something they hadn't shared in months. But now here she was, on her knees, crying and talking to a God he could not see or feel. A god who in George's mind, had never helped them.

"All I wanted was one night," he muttered under his breath. "One night to see if we could fix this. And here she is, choosing God over me again."

George's anger boiled over. "Then wait on Him in the living room!" George snapped, yanking the covers off the bed. "I'm trying to sleep, Jenny."

Jenny turned, startled, tears still running down her face.

"I'm trying to sleep," George repeated, louder now, his voice cutting. "And you're in here praying to a god who doesn't even exist! You're selfish as hell. You asked me to come home and I did. And now you won't even let me sleep. How selfish is that, Jenny?"

Jenny stood, reaching for him. "George, please—"

But for the first time, he pushed her away. The force sent her stumbling backward, and only then did he notice how thin she had become. It barely took a push to knock her off balance. But George was too angry to care.

"You know what?" he spat. "I'll go to the living room. I can't stand to be in your presence right now. You make me sick. I'm beginning to hate you and everything you believe in." George stormed out of the bedroom, and slammed the door behind him.

Jenny stood frozen for a moment, then collapsed onto the bed in sobs.

She reached for a spare sheet in the dresser and wrapped it around herself, shaking uncontrollably.

"There's no need, Jesus," she whispered. "He hates me. God, what do I do? He doesn't love me anymore. He treats me like a stranger. I tried, Lord. I really tried. I don't want to do this anymore. I know there's someone else. I'm sure of it. I just...I just want to give up."

Jenny buried her face in the pillow and wept until her whole body ached. And then, softly, she heard Him again.

"This too shall pass. Be patient. I will avenge you, Jenny. I will deal with your adversary."

Her tears slowed as His words wrapped around her like a blanket, even as her heart broke.

Johnny had heard the shouting and the sound of the bedroom door slamming.

He got out of bed and padded down the hallway, stopping when he saw his father stretched out on the couch, muttering under his breath.

From down the hall, he could hear soft, muffled sobs coming from behind his mother's bedroom door.

What did this idiot do now? Johnny thought bitterly. *He always makes Mom cry.*

"Mom, you okay?" Johnny called through the door.

George lifted his head. "Go back to bed, John. Your mother's praying."

But Johnny wasn't stupid. He knew the difference between his mother's prayers and her tears.

He ignored his father and knocked again. "Momma? You okay?"

When there was no answer, Johnny quietly opened the door. His chest tightened when he saw her lying on the bed, wrapped in nothing but a sheet, her face wet with tears. Johnny's anger at his father burned hot in his chest. He walked over to the bed and climbed in beside her, lying down without saying a word. He wanted so badly to tell her what he'd discovered about George; the cheating, the lies, but he knew it would break her. Instead, he wrapped an arm around her.

"Mommy, it's gonna be okay," he whispered. Jenny lifted her head slightly, looking at her son. She hated that Johnny knew. She hated that he had to witness any of this. But she didn't have the strength to pretend tonight. She rested her head against Johnny's chest, letting him hold her.

Within minutes, she drifted off to sleep, tears still clinging to her lashes. Johnny stared up at the ceiling, holding his mother tight. He wished he were more like GT. His big brother would've shown George a thing or two for making their mom cry. Eventually, Johnny's own eyes grew heavy, and he fell asleep with his mother in his arms. Johnny determined that one day, he would protect her the way GT would have.

In the stillness of that night, Jenny's tears spoke a language Heaven understood. The sting of George's words hung heavy in the air, each one cutting deeper than the last. Her heart ached, not only from his cruelty, but from the silence she felt from the God she loved. It seemed as though the walls were closing in — the room, the marriage, the life she once knew.

Loneliness pressed in, whispering that this was all she would ever know. But in the unseen realm, the Lord was nearer than her breath. God was watching, listening, holding her fragile spirit in His hands. Every insult, every cold word, every lonely moment was being gathered, redeemed, and woven into a greater story. A story where joy will rise from ashes, and love will embrace her again. This battle is not her ending. It is the sacred beginning of her becoming.

Chapter 10

Rick sat slumped over his desk, his head resting on his arms. He was exhausted. It was not just physically, but mentally. Yesterday's rendezvous with Paula still had him twisted. He felt disgusted with himself for letting things go that far. But he also felt...satisfied. Too satisfied. It was a feeling he hadn't had in years. It both thrilled and terrified him.

The office door swung open, and George walked in "Man, you look worn out," George said, shaking his head.

"I am," Rick admitted, sitting up and rubbing his face.

George chuckled and sat across from him. "I know that young girl's wearing you out. And I know it's sick. You're still messing around with that seventeen-year-old? I thought you said you were trying to end it."

Rick shifted in his seat, suddenly uncomfortable.

"Believe me, I've tried," he said with a humorless laugh. "But she's under my skin, George. This girl...she puts it down like she's forty. I never had a woman like this."

Rick felt his stomach knot as he spoke. Every time he mentioned Paula, even indirectly, he worried that one day he'd slip and say too much. If George ever found out the truth, Rick knew he wouldn't live to tell about it. George leaned back in his chair, shaking his head. "You know what goes down, Rick, always comes back up," George said, his tone hard. "If it was my daughter, you'd already be in a casket. The only reason your ass ain't in jail right now is because I don't know who this girl is. I have a sixteen and a half year-old daughter, Rick. How would you feel if some old dude was laying up with Paula? How would you feel being around her?"

Rick felt his mouth go dry. He forced a laugh. "I feel good. I feel..." He caught himself just in time and quickly straightened his face, taking the grin off before it could betray him.

George looked up from his phone, his expression suddenly sharp.

"You feel what?" George asked, his voice dangerously calm. "Man, you looking at my daughter like what?"

Rick held up his hands defensively. "Stop playing, George. You know Paula's like a niece to me. I would never touch Paula."

He lied smoothly, praying George couldn't see through him. Rick had always been afraid of George. He'd seen firsthand what George was capable of. Rick wasn't about to confess to something that would sign his death warrant. George's eyes narrowed as he leaned across the desk.

"I know this much Rick, if I ever find out some bull, not only does our friendship end, but so does your life." George glared at him. "This is sickening. You know what this makes you look like? A damn pervert. You know this is wrong, Rick. Sleeping with a girl that young?"

Rick leaned back, startled. George was angry, but there was something sharper in his tone this time. Something else was bothering him.

"Wait one damn minute," Rick said, straightening up. "Hold on. You really sitting here judging me right now?"

George's glare hardened. "No, you wait one minute," George snapped. "I told you from the beginning that you needed to confess. This girl was just sixteen then. I didn't agree with it then and I don't agree with it now. I got a daughter, Rick."

Rick's voice grew sharper. "And you got a wife. The pot calling the kettle black, huh? Jenny is a beautiful, intelligent, wise woman. And you're out here messing with Cassandra, a chick who ain't got nothing going for her but some head."

George's mouth dropped open. "Are you serious right now? Are you really trying to compare what I'm doing with a grown woman to you sleeping with someone barely out of high school?"

George shook his head in disbelief.

"You are the last person I'd take advice from." Rick leaned forward, his anger matched George's. "Yes, I mess with a seventeen-year-old, but she's not married. You know how I feel every time I'm around Jenny, knowing what you're doing with Cassandra? I've covered you for eight years, George. Not for you, but for Jenny's sake."

"And guess what? Every woman I was with was grown, consenting adults. I wasn't breaking any laws. You can't sit here and tell me you feel good about what you're doing right now, because I see it all over your face."

Rick fell silent for a beat.

"The fact you brought this up," George continued but his voice lowered, "lets me know you don't agree with it either."

Rick rubbed his face with both hands. "You don't think I know it's wrong? You don't think I've tried to end it? I sound pathetic right now, but I swear to you, I am going to end it. I am not as sick as you think I am."

George let out a bitter laugh. "Hmm, mmm. Until your penis says otherwise. Man, this girl got your head buried in the sand."

Rick rubbed his face and groaned. "I've tried ending it, George. I really have. But every time I do, she...she pulls me back in. Sex is...man, it's unreal. I've never had a woman put it down like this girl. She gives me head. This girl is a freak. She did something to me no other could." He let out a shaky laugh, almost ashamed.

"She took my player card, man. No woman's ever done that before."

"What's wrong with you?" George stared at him, his expression turning cold.

Rick shook his head. "She made me cry during sex, George. Cry. She does these tricks with her vagina." "Stop. I don't want to hear it." George shot up a hand, cutting him off. "She is a baby. And none of this—"

George gestured angrily toward him "None of this turns me on or impresses me. I've got a sixteen year-old daughter. If it was my daughter, Rick? You wouldn't be talking to me right now. You'd be feeling the spirit of death, along with some lead from my gun."

Rick swallowed hard, fear flashing across his face. "I know. That's why I'm trying to end it. I swear I am. I'm terrified of her father. I've always been.

"You're right, George. I know it's wrong. I'm not proud of this. I hate myself for it. But I feel trapped. And I don't know how to get out."

George leaned forward suddenly, making Rick flinch. Then he punched him hard in the shoulder.

"Man up," George said, his voice hard. "Man up, Rick. End it before it ends you."

For a moment, they sat in tense silence. George loved Rick like a brother. But, he had no respect for him.

Chapter 11

The kitchen gleamed with life. There were slick countertops, stainless steel appliances shining under the warm recessed lights, and a mosaic backsplash that seemed to glow. The faint aroma of spices from last night's cooking still hung in the air.

Juanita and Jenny sat at the kitchen table, steaming mugs of coffee between them. Jenny admired her mother-in-law deeply. Juanita had been more of a mother to her than her own ever was. She could talk to her about anything, even about George. Juanita would always be honest. She was never biased, always quick to point out Jenny's mistakes gently, to correct her softly when she needed it, and to drop everything if Jenny needed her.

"Thanks for coming over, Mom," Jenny said quietly. Juanita smiled as she twirled her new car keys between her fingers. "I had to break in my new wheels," she teased. "I know you talked George into buying me this car." She reached across the table and touched Jenny's arm.

"Besides, I needed to talk to you. How are you doing?"

Jenny hesitated, then nodded, her voice trembling. "I know, Mom. I know you can feel it. I know what I know."

Juanita's smile faded, her eyes narrowing slightly. "You know what?" she asked gently. She had already guessed where this conversation would go. Jenny's tears began to fall as she stared at her mother-in-law. "George is having an affair," she said, her voice breaking.

"I feel it in my spirit. I know it for sure. I'm tired of crying, tired of praying for what feels like a dead situation. Your son is a liar and a cheater, and I'm tired of all the lies he tells. He thinks I don't know he's messing around, but I'm no fool."

Juanita reached for Jenny's hand, her heart ached. How could she defend George? She couldn't. This was what George Sr. had done to her, and now she saw herself in Jenny. She had endured the same pain and the same heartbreak.

"A woman always knows," Juanita said softly. "I knew. And I won't sit here and tell you that what you feel is wrong. All I can say is this...I knew when George Sr. was cheating on me."

Jenny grabbed a napkin from the table and wiped her tears. "How did you handle it, Mom? I've been through this before with George, but I can't keep doing this all my life."

Juanita gave a short, dry laugh. "Handle it? Girl, the police were at our house so much you'd think we lived at the precinct."

Jenny let out a small laugh through her tears.

"I busted out car windows, burned down apartments," Juanita said with a shake of her head. "Girl, no. I didn't handle it well at all, not at all. I was angry most of the time. We fought constantly. There were plenty of restless nights in that house."

"But you stayed with him. Why?" Jenny asked softly.

"Probably the same reason I stay with George," she admitted. "I don't know why I put up with his disrespectful and cheating ways. I feel trapped. Unwanted. George is all I have. Where would I even go?"

Juanita reached across the table and touched Jenny's arm. "Listen to me, baby. I didn't stay because I wanted to. At first, I thought I could change him. Then, after a while, I just felt stuck. I felt like I had no choice. With five kids? Who was going to want me? So I stayed."

Jenny shook her head, confused. "Mom, why did you feel like that? You're a beautiful woman. I've seen pictures of you back in the day. Even when I first met you, I couldn't believe how gorgeous you were. Any man would have wanted you back then."

Juanita's eyes softened, but there was pain behind them. "Jenny," she said quietly, "I'm about to tell you something I've never told another soul. My mother died before I could tell her.

The only other person who knows is George, because he was the one who told me."

Juanita stood, poured Jenny another cup of coffee, then sat back down across from her.

Jenny reached for her hand. "Mom, you can tell me anything."

Juanita hesitated for a long moment before speaking. "I'm HIV positive," she said at last, her voice barely above a whisper.

"I've been living with the virus for over ten years now."

Jenny gasped, her hand flying to her mouth. "Mom, wait. Are you telling me you have AIDS?" Her voice broke as tears welled in her eyes.

"Shh." Juanita squeezed her hand gently. "No, not full-blown AIDS. I take care of myself, Jenny. I take my medicine faithfully, and I live a healthy life."

Jenny wiped her eyes, trying to process what she just heard. "George knows this?" she asked quietly. "You said he told you...How?"

"Yes, George knows. He was the one who told me." Juanita nodded. "Let me explain. Remember when George started handling his father's business after he passed? I didn't know anything until George got the death certificate."

Jenny stared at her, stunned, trying to process the weight of what she was saying. "What do you mean you didn't know until George got the death certificate?"

Juanita sighed, folding her hands on the table.

"What I mean is this, George Sr. knew he was sick. He was on medication. George found the bottles when he was cleaning out the garage, hidden in a toolbox behind the shed." Her voice softened.

"George Sr. never told me, Jenny. Not once. Sure, I'd get a few colds, sometimes felt like I had the flu, but that was it. Never in a million years would I have thought to take an HIV test. Not at my age. I had been married for over thirty years. I never cheated. I wasn't thinking..." Jaunita shook her head.

"I wasn't thinking at all. But the fact is, George Sr. was out there cheating. I should have protected myself. I should have protected George, too."

Jenny squeezed her hand, tears in her eyes. "You can't possibly blame yourself for this, Mom. This isn't your fault."

Juanita nodded slowly. "No, baby. I don't blame myself anymore. I went through that phase. I've experienced all the guilt, and all the rage. It took me ten years after George Sr.'s death to forgive him. And most importantly, to forgive myself. I was angry. So angry I could barely breathe. But I let it go. I forgave him. I forgave myself. And I'm not mad anymore."

Jenny shook her head, stunned. "Wow, Mom. I never knew. You look so healthy."

Juanita smiled faintly. "It took me a long time to come to grips with it, to understand this isn't a death sentence. You can live beyond the diagnosis. George...Well, George is another story. I still don't know if he's ever really accepted that I'm positive. The day he read his father's death certificate and found out George Sr. was HIV positive...it changed him. Changed our relationship too."

When George Sr. died, he and Juanita were no longer living as husband and wife. She had nowhere to go. Juanita had no money to get her own place. George Sr. had controlled all the finances during their marriage and left her with no access to anything.

Juanita had begged him to move out of the family home, but he refused. He wouldn't help her get a place of her own either. So, she temporarily moved in with George and Jenny. But night after night, George Sr. would show up at their house, pounding on the door and demanding she come home. He said he was sick and needed her.

Eventually, Juanita agreed to return, but only under one condition: that they would not live as husband and wife. He agreed.

Jenny shook her head, tears in her eyes. "I wouldn't know what that's like. Your son doesn't talk to me, doesn't touch me. Half the time, he doesn't even look at me unless it's a death stare or to ask for food.

"I don't know why he hates me so much. I don't know what I did to him." Juanita sighed, getting up to pour them both another cup of coffee.

"I don't believe he hates you," she said softly. "And maybe...maybe he doesn't even realize how distant he's become."

Jenny stared into her mug. "I've tried so many times to talk to him. But he says I'm nagging. I don't even know if he's noticed I've lost weight. Honestly, I don't even know if he sees me at all anymore." Juanita sat back down and placed a gentle hand on Jenny's.

"Are you praying, Jenny?"

Jenny nodded weakly. "I am. But not like I used to. I've been so tired lately. Just dragging around the house." She let out a shaky breath. "I made a doctor's appointment. I'll see him next week."

Before Juanita could respond, the kitchen door swung open and Johnny stepped in.

"Hey, Grandmamma!" he said, grinning.

Johnny leaned down and planted a kiss on Juanita's cheek.

"Hey, John-John," Juanita smiled, her face lighting up. "Do Grandmama a favor, sweetie."

Johnny straightened proudly. "Anything for you, Grand!"

Juanita looked Johnny up and down, shaking her head. "Pull up your pants, boy. I don't know how you think that looks good. Don't you feel uncomfortable?" Johnny grinned and hiked them up. Jenny laughed.

"Wow, Mom! I need you around all the time. I get on him about that constantly. He just tells me it's 'today's fashion.'"

Juanita waved her hand dismissively. "It wouldn't be the fashion in my house. He'd pull up his pants before he came through my doors. George never wore his pants like that. None of your uncles did."

Johnny smirked. "Dad, that was back in your day, Grandmama. Y'all didn't know fashion back then."

Juanita's head snapped toward him playfully. "Excuse me? We were the fashion, honey! What? Do you call this fashion? Walking around with your pants halfway off your behind? There's no fashion in showing your underwear."

Johnny couldn't help but laugh. "Yeah, yeah. I know. Y'all were Gucci back in the day."

Juanita grinned, proud. "If you mean the bomb, that's right. And don't you forget it! Yes! The bomb.'

She stood and grabbed her purse. "Jenny, I better get going before it gets too dark. You know my eyesight ain't what it used to be at night."

Johnny chuckled. "Or in the morning...or afternoon either." He laughed at his own joke.

Juanita balled her fist playfully and air-punched at him. "What you say, boy!"

"Nothing, Grandmama. Just get home safe," Johnny said quickly, grinning. He bent down and kissed her cheek.

"Mama Juanita, I'll call you later," Jenny said, standing. "John-John, help your grandmother to the car, please."

"Okay, Mommy. You ready to go, Grandma?" Johnny asked, offering her his hand.

Juanita hugged Jenny before leaving. "I really need you to make that doctor's appointment. You're looking a little thin and worn down. Please promise me you'll see a doctor."

"I promise. I already did. I will see him next week," Jenny reassured her and turned to Johnny. "I'm going to lie down. When you come back in, make sure you wash your hands before you go into my pots or the fridge."

"I will," Johnny said with a nod as he walked his grandmother out to the car.

Chapter 12

With barely a sliver of moonlight peeking through the curtains, Cassandra's bedroom was a pool of deep shadows. The wrinkled white sheets glowed softly in the dim light, evidence of what had just taken place. George laid back and breathed heavily as sweat cooled on his skin. He needed this. Needed her. After what had happened with Jenny, after the argument, after the way she looked at him. He needed to blow off steam. But Cassandra wasn't smiling.

"I'm not playing with you, George. I'm tired of this arrangement. I'm fed up." George leaned down, kissed her stomach, trying to soften her. "You don't think I'm tired too? I'm fed up as well."

Cassandra pushed him off. "I can't tell. Looks to me like you've got your cake. And you're eating it all by yourself."

George sat up on one elbow, his jaw tight. "I keep telling you. It's complicated. I can't leave Jenny like that. She's fragile right now. Her mother just died."

"A year ago," Cassandra rolled her eyes. She started to climb out of bed, but George grabbed her wrist and pulled her back.

"Yes, a year ago and she was very close to her mother. Despite everything, my wife is a good woman." George didn't mention that Jenny and her mother had been estranged. Cassandra didn't need to know that.

Cassandra glared at him. "If she's such a good woman, why are you here with me?"

George didn't answer right away.

"Because my feelings have changed," he said finally, his voice low. "I'm not in love with her anymore. I'm in love with you."

George moved over her, pinning her beneath him. Cassandra pushed against his chest.

"Then divorce her. If you love me, divorce her. Either you end this marriage, or I'm gone. Me...and the baby." George froze.

Cassandra stared at him, unblinking. She had loved George once. Loved him so much that, when she became pregnant, she went through with getting rid of the baby because he told her to. But that was the day she knew he would never leave Jenny. All bets were off. George opened his mouth to answer. "I will and I am," he started to say, but Cassandra shook her head.

"You've been saying that for eight years, George. Eight years. And every year, there's something new. I'm 28 and you still have the same excuses. Last year it was because her mother died. This year it's because she's 'too fragile.' I'm done being dragged along."

"I love you, Sandy," George said, his voice low. "You know that, right? You already know why I can't just get up and leave Jenny without clearing some loose ends. I can't afford to lose everything I've worked so hard to build."

Cassandra crossed her arms, her expression flat. "I think you love what you can get from me."

George sat up, frustrated. "I can't stand to be in her presence anymore. Why do you think I'm always over here?" Cassandra glared at him.

"Yeah, let's discuss that. You only come after dark. We never eat dinner together. And every Sunday, you're at home with her. For a man who never goes to church, you sure do make sure you're home on Sunday."

George smirked. "That's because you can't cook. Jenny can throw down in the kitchen. I've got to get my eat on."

He shook his head. "I'm sick of hearing you complain. You knew the situation when you first came into this. I laid it all out from the beginning. Now, you want to change the rules."

Cassandra's voice rose. "I didn't know it would take this long for you to leave your wife! You've had me dangling for years, George."

George had a company holiday party and Cassandra was part of the catering service staff for the night. She knew a little background about George because her one of friends also had an affair with him. Cassandra liked how George carried himself. He was very sexy to her. She met Jenny that night and admired how beautiful Jenny was but she wanted what she wanted. No one would stand in the way.

Cassandra loved George at first but when she became pregnant and George made her get rid of the baby she knew then he would never leave Jenny. All bets were off. Cassandra was going to use George and get all she could. She knew it is wrong to mess around with a married man. She knew what the scriptures said about adulterers. Cassandra was a preacher's kid but she didn't care. There was no conviction on her part because she knew George was full of it. Cassandra also knew she was not the only woman George was laying up with.

Though she was five foot three, slim with hips and big breasts due to plastic surgery, Cassandra felt worthless. George was never going to choose her. Even if he did, Cassandra's father didn't want his precious white daughter with a black man. This relationship would never be accepted by her family.

"Let's get something clear. Did I ever tell you I'd leave my wife? George's jaw tightened. "No matter what, I told you I had a lot invested in my marriage. So, stop pressing me. It will happen when it happens."

Cassandra shoved him off her. "When is that, George?"

"It will happen when it happens," he repeated, rubbing her belly.

Cassandra tensed up in anger and slapped his hand away. George reached out and rubbed Cassandra's belly once again, this time more deliberately.

"When is your doctor's appointment? Have you even made one?"

Cassandra jerked back and slapped his hand away once again. "Doctor's appointment?" she repeated, annoyed. "For what?"

George's tone hardened. "For the baby, Cassandra. The baby."

Cassandra looked away. "Oh…I had to reschedule," she lied.

"Again? That's the third time. I want to make sure everything's fine." George stared at her.

Cassandra rolled her eyes. "Everything is fine, George. If it wasn't, you would've known by now."

"How?" George snapped. "You haven't been to a doctor once since you found out you were pregnant."

He reached for her belly again. Cassandra turned to him quickly, pressing her lips to his neck and chest, eager to change the subject.

"Oh, baby. Now, come here." George gave in, pulling her closer.

"I'll make the appointment," she whispered, trailing kisses across his jaw. "I promise, sweetie. I'll let you know."

"You do that," George murmured, flipping her onto her back. He kissed her neck, then her breasts.

Cassandra giggled as he grabbed her hips. "I love you, George," she said breathlessly. "I want all of you. Every day. From your head…"

Her hand slid down his stomach until she cupped him. "…to the monster man," she teased.

"I want every inch of you. I don't want Jenny to have anything that belongs to me. Every bit of you is mine."

George's eyes darkened. "Then take all of me," he growled, flipping her onto her back.

Cassandra's lips curled into a slow, satisfied smile. This was what she wanted. Cassandra desired all of him. Outside, the night was quiet, the moonlight spilling through the curtains. Inside, the room filled with breathless laughter, whispered promises, and the sound of two people clinging to something they both knew was dangerous. But as George buried himself in her. A single thought clawed at the back of his mind. No matter how much he gave to Cassandra, a part of him still belonged to Jenny. And that part refused to let go.

Chapter 13

The kitchen smelled of freshly baked bread and a hint of herbs drifting in from the garden outside. Morning sunlight streamed through the huge window, lighting up the polished oak counters. A bowl of colorful fruit sat in the middle, adding a cheerful splash of color.

Jenny stood at the stove. She tried to finish breakfast but was barely holding herself upright.

"I'm so tired," she muttered, sliding into the chair next to Paula. "I don't know why I feel so worn down. My God...I'm drained."

Paula frowned, reaching out to touch her mother's cheek. "Yeah, Mom, you don't look so good. Are you feeling okay?"

Paula had always admired her mother's beauty. But, today she could see something was wrong. Jenny looked thinner. Too thin.

"I was feeling a little bad yesterday," Jenny admitted. "But this morning…I feel worse."

Jenny leaned back, silently thanking God she didn't hit the floor first.

"You didn't rest too well last night, Mommy?" Johnny said from the kitchen. He sat his Nintendo 3DS down and came over to her side.

"How did you sleep last night?" he added.

"I should've slept just fine," Jenny said. "Your father didn't get in until this morning. I had the entire bed to myself."

Johnny smirked. "Let me guess. He 'had to work late.'"

Paula rolled her eyes. *That's a lie,* she thought.

Johnny bent down, sticking his tongue out toward Jenny's forehead like he was checking her temperature. She swatted at him playfully.

"You feel a little warm, Mom. Maybe you're coming down with the flu. You should see a doctor."

"Yeah," Jenny nodded weakly. "I think I will, much sooner than planned."

Paula crossed her arms. "Good idea. You've been acting a little weird lately."

"If anyone knows weird, it's you," Johnny teased.

"Shut up, butt-breath. You always have something stupid to say with your fat head self," Paula shot back.

Johnny grinned. "Sliding board. Roller coaster."

Paula whipped her head toward him, glaring. "Sliding board? That's low…even for you."

Jenny shot him a look. "John-John, watch your mouth and apologize to your sister. That's not nice." She didn't like when the twins spoke to each other that way, even if it was joking.

Johnny rolled his eyes but kissed his mother's cheek. "Fine. I apologize, ugly."

Paula smirked. "You know about rides. Don't you give your homeboys full rides?"

"Paula!" Jenny coughed and smacked her daughter's hand lightly. "Both of you: enough."

Jenny's heart ached. As much as they fought, she admired them both. She remembered how she and George wrestled over Paula's name. Jenny had wanted Johnanne — a tribute to her grandfather John and favorite aunt Anne. George had wanted Paula. In the end, she thought she'd won with Johnanne Paula…until her daughter grew up and refused to answer to anything but Paula. Another battle lost to George.

Before Jenny could say more, the bedroom door opened. George stepped out, his presence filling the kitchen. He didn't notice Jenny's pale face or the tension between the twins. George was hungry.

"Where's my breakfast?" he barked.

Jenny stood up quietly and went to make him a plate.

Paula leaned toward him and whispered, "Mommy's not feeling good today, Daddy."

George ignored her.

"If you'd stay your ass home sometimes, maybe you wouldn't feel so worn out," he said to Jenny. "Every time I turn around, you're running with those holy rollers. Now you wonder why you're so sick."

Johnny slammed his hand on the table. "Pops, how would you know what Mommy's doing? You're not home enough to even recognize her at all."

George stopped cold, turned, and stood over Johnny, his jaw tight. "Who are you talking to like that?"

Jenny turned toward her son, her voice firm but tired. "John-John, be respectful."

But Johnny didn't budge. His jaw tightened. He could see his mother was too weak to respond to George. Johnny decided he would respond for her.

"No, Mom. I'm sick of this."

He turned toward his father, his voice rising. "I'm sick and tired of the way you talk to her. All Mommy does is cook, clean, take care of your business, go to church, and take care of us and you? You're killing her, and you don't even care!"

Johnny's chair scraped loudly against the floor as he stood.

"Watch your mouth, boy. Watch who you're talking to." George woke up angry and Johnny's little stunt was just what he needed.

Johnny stood toe to toe with his father now. He refused to look away.

"No. You watch your mouth!" Johnny's chest rose and fell with anger.

"All you ever do is disrespect my mother. You've been doing it for years. Can't you see how much weight she's lost? If she's worn out, it's because of you and all the bullshit you put her through. Tell me. What time did you even come in last night? The only time you show up here is for breakfast, lunch, and dinner!"

George's expression shifted. He stepped forward, reaching for Johnny, but Johnny jumped back just in time. George's fists clenched, his eyes blazing. George's voice thundered through the kitchen.

"Boy, as long as you live under my roof, don't you ever disrespect me or talk to me like that again!"

Jenny quickly grabbed George's arm. She tried to calm him, but he yanked it away. Paula stayed quiet, wide-eyed, secretly relieved someone was finally saying what she'd been too afraid to say.

Johnny stepped closer to his mother, his voice low and sharp. "Careful, Father. We wouldn't want the light to shine, would we?"

George froze, his eyes narrowing. Slowly, he sat back down. Johnny leaned against the counter casually, as if daring him.

"You know, I met this girl the other day: Cassandra. She said, 'You look so familiar.' I told her, 'I bet I do.'"

Jenny turned, confused. "Really? Who is this girl, John-John? You have a new love now?"

She looked at George. "Where did you meet this one from?"

George broke eye contact with Jenny. Johnny shook his head.

"Oh no, Mom…not me. She knows one of my homeboy's girls. And guess what? She's pregnant."

Jenny's heart skipped. "Which homeboy? Do I know him?"

As soon as the words left her mouth, she caught George's expression. The subtle shift in his face, the way his temper cooled instantly.

Jenny's breath caught. "What's wrong, dear? Is something wrong?"

George snapped, his voice harsh. "Why are you asking me a stupid question? Don't you see your son disrespecting me? And you have the nerve to ask me what's wrong?"

Jenny stared at him, her gut twisting. Oh, she knew exactly what was wrong. He could pretend this was about Johnny's attitude, but Jenny could see through him. She turned to Johnny. "John-John, you said I know him, right?"

Johnny smirked. "Yeah. You know him very, very well."

George exhaled sharply and sat back in his chair. He reached into his pocket and pulled out a wad of cash.

"How much is this fitted, John-John? How much do you want?" He was desperate now, determined to change the subject. George was so confused and so terrified that Johnny might actually expose him that he forgot he'd already given Johnny money for the fitted.

George threw two hundred dollars across the table. Jenny stared at him, her anger boiling.

"How are you feeling, dear?" George asked, his voice suddenly soft.

Jenny's lips trembled. "I don't feel good," she said flatly. "I've been feeling bad for two months."

George's eyes flicked to Johnny, who tilted his head with a knowing look. George cleared his throat. "Have you been to the doctor, dear?"

That was it. Jenny slapped him hard across the face.

"No, asshole, I haven't!" she screamed.

Everyone went silent. Jenny stood tall, tears streaming down her face. "Look here, I'm not playing these games anymore. John-John, you can stop blackmailing your father now. I already know about Cassandra. I already know your dad has been seeing another woman. I already know about the white whore he's been sneaking around with for the last eight years!"

George's hand went to his cheek, his face a mask of shock. "Wh-what?" he stammered.

Jenny stepped closer, her voice steady but ice cold. "Yeah, George. I know. I've known for years.

"You know what bothers me more than finding out you were still messing with her after you promised me you'd stop?"

Her voice cracked, but she didn't back down. "It's that you looked me in my face, swore on our children, and still chose her over your family."

Jenny turned sharply to Johnny, her voice trembling but fierce. "And you!"

Her eyes filled with tears as she pointed at her son. "You knew. You knew and instead of coming to me, you blackmailed your father. Where is your love for me, John-John?"

Johnny's mouth fell open, but he didn't say a word. Paula glanced between them, frozen in shock.

Jenny broke down, tears streaming down her face. She spun on her heel, stormed out of the kitchen, and returned moments later holding a stack of papers. Without a word, she threw them at George. "I'm done."

George caught the papers, confused. "What is this?"

He flipped to the first page and his eyes widening when he realized what he was holding.

"A divorce?" he stammered, looking up at her.

"Wait...Jenny, wait!"

Jenny's voice cracked, but she stood firm. "I want a divorce, George."

George stared at her, stunned. His mouth worked but no sound came out at first.

"What...what...what?" he muttered, shaking his head in disbelief.

Jenny slammed a DVD on the table next to the divorce papers.

"And since that apartment your whore is living in is under the company name," she said coldly, "I had cameras installed in every room.

"There are years of footage, George! Years of your extramarital affairs.

"And just in case you thought I was bluffing...I had your office under surveillance too."

Paula couldn't help it, she laughed. For the first time in years, she saw the old Jenny, the no-nonsense woman from the block.

"Let's see how Daddy gets out of this one," she muttered under her breath.

Jenny turned to George, her voice shaking but steady. "So you can't lie this time, dear. I put up with your mess for years. I worked three jobs to put you through college, helped build this business from the ground up. And this is what I get?"

Her knees felt weak, and she sank into a chair. Johnny stepped forward to comfort her, but she pulled away, lowering her head to the table.

Paula reached out, touching her mother's hand gently. "Mom...you okay?"

Jenny lifted her tear-stained face and glared at George, her eyes blazing.

"This," she said, holding up the DVD, "is a video of your whore.

"And you're going to find out real quick, honey. You're not the only one Cassandra's been with. She's been banging half the city...even some of your so-called homeboys. So go ahead, watch it. See how special you really are."

George's face was drained of color. "How do you even know...I mean, you don't—"

Jenny cut him off, her voice rising. "I don't what, George? I don't know that you're a liar? A cheater? That you're just like your father? You saw what your dad did to your mom. You saw what she went through. And you still put me through the same hell."

Her tears flowed and her voice was so calm it was chilling.

"It doesn't even matter anymore. I don't hate you, George. I'm through that stage. I'm not even mad at you. I actually feel sorry for you because while you thought you were playing me, you were the one getting played." Jenny laughed bitterly, shaking her head.

"My God, the same one you despise, is the only reason you're still breathing. He stopped me so many times from slipping rat poison in your food. You honestly would have left me for that slut. But here's the kicker, George! You were never as slick as you thought you were. I know about all of them. Every single woman. Even the ones you took to your office. And the only difference between me and your mother is…today we have technology."

Jenny shoved back from the table, stormed out of the kitchen, and disappeared into her bedroom. Moments later, the sound of her sobbing echoed down the hallway. Johnny stared at his father, shaking his head. "I pray she takes you for everything you're worth…which ain't much." He slammed the money back onto the table and left to check on his mother.

George sat there, shell-shocked, staring at the divorce papers and videotape in front of him. He ran a hand down his face.

"What am I gonna do?" he whispered, almost to himself. He turned to Paula, desperate for some kind of answer. But Paula just shrugged.

"Guess the cat's out of the bag, Daddy."

George stared down at the divorce papers again, flipping through them in disbelief. He shook his head slowly.

"I don't understand. I thought I had everything covered. How did she—" He looked up at Paula, almost pleading. He asked once again. "What am I going to do?"

Paula crossed her arms, her face cold. She stood to check on her mother. "Kiss your ass goodbye, Daddy. This is what happens when you mess around with a whore."

She took a step toward the door, then turned back with a cruel smirk.

"Oh! And guess what? That baby isn't even yours. That chick isn't pregnant." Paula laughed, shaking her head as she walked out of the kitchen to check on Jenny. Inside, though, something in her shifted.

She had always had trust issues with men, but this; this was proof that she was right all along. Her father had just justified every wall she'd built around herself. She lost whatever little respect she had left for him that day. And now, more than ever, Paula was determined to treat men exactly the way she believed they deserved to be treated. She vowed to break them down before they ever had a chance to hurt her.

Chapter 14

Jenny laid on the bed and cried uncontrollably. The grief felt heavier than ever. Betrayal pressed on her chest until she could barely breathe. Every thought of George and Cassandra sent another wave of pain through her. She wasn't just heartbroken. Jenny was consumed with sadness and rage. Paula slipped quietly into the room. Johnny was already there, sitting close to his mother, trying to comfort her.

"Mommy, I'm sorry," Johnny said, his voice cracking. "I didn't mean to hurt you. I thought by not telling you, it would be better. I didn't want to see you cry like this."

Jenny lifted her tear-streaked face, staring at her son. "Then why did you blackmail your father, John-John? I can't understand that. Why blackmail him?"

Johnny swallowed hard, his shoulders slumped over. "Mommy, it wasn't about the money. I thought if I pushed him, it would change him. I thought he'd stop. I just wanted him to be better for you."

Jenny shook her head, fresh tears sliding down her cheeks.

Paula shook her head at Johnny. "This family has too many secrets. Just a bunch of lies. If you knew he was cheating, and you had all the evidence, why stay with Daddy?"

"Because I thought he still loved me." Jenny's voice softened. "And yet, here I am. Broken anyway."

Jenny leaned back against the headboard. She lowered her head and spoke to Johnny through tears. "I stayed with him because I prayed. John-John. I hoped...no, I begged God that one day your father would change. But I never thought he'd get this woman pregnant. That was the final straw."

Paula knelt next to the bed, lifting her mother's chin gently. "She's not pregnant, Mom. She's lying."

Jenny's lips trembled. "I know she's not now. But there was a time she was."

Paula froze. "What?"

"Your grandmother helped her get an abortion," Jenny whispered.

Paula blinked in disbelief. "Grandma? Why didn't anyone tell me?"

Jenny's face hardened. "Because not every secret needs to be another scar, Paula. I was trying to protect you two."

Paula bit her lip, feeling guilty, but she nodded. "I just...found out yesterday," She lied, not wanting to add to her mother's pain.

The bedroom door creaked open. George stepped inside, his face tense as he held the divorce papers. "Please," he said quietly. "Let me have a few minutes with your mother."

He touched Paula's shoulder. She jerked away from him.

"Let me speak with her," George said, glancing at Johnny.

Both twins gave him a look of death. Johnny leaned toward Jenny. "Mom, are you okay with this?"

Jenny nodded weakly. "Yes, John-John. I'm okay."

Johnny kissed her forehead. "I'll be right outside the door. Call me if you need me."

He turned to his father. "My mom's been through enough, Dad."

Paula kissed Jenny's cheek. "I'll be in the family room, Mom. Just call me if you need me."

George closed the door after they left and sat on the bed beside Jenny. He reached for her hand, but she pulled back.

"Jenny," George started, his voice low, "I never meant to hurt you. I—"

Jenny cut him off. "Please, George. That's exactly what you meant to do. I heard you. I heard every conversation. Every time you told that woman you hated me, that you hated being in the same room with me. That you hated touching me. You never meant not to get caught. You just never thought I'd be smart enough to find out."

George's voice grew desperate. "Then you should've heard me say I would never leave you."

Jenny's bitter laugh filled the room. "Oh, I heard that too. The many times you told Rick you'd never divorce me because you were too afraid of losing your money. I loved you, George. I really did. But I can't do this any longer. I deserve better than this. I deserve better than you."

George flinched at her words. "Loved?" His voice cracked. "Are you saying you don't love me anymore?"

Jenny stared at him coldly. "Now you're worried about my love for you? Why, George? Because I asked for a divorce?"

"No," he said quickly. "Because I still love you."

Jenny stood from the bed. "Really, George? You're only saying that now because you got caught. I'm not your fool anymore." She shook her head as a small, humorless laugh slipped out.

"No! This isn't about love. This is about control. And for the first time in my life, George…"

Jenny stepped back, standing taller, her tears drying on her cheeks. "I am putting my foot down. You don't get to gaslight me anymore. You don't get to twist my feelings or make me second-guess myself. I'm done letting you play with my heart. I'm done with your narcissistic games."

George stood too, reaching for her. "I'm not playing games, Jenny. I mean it." George's desperation rose.

"Then sign the papers."

Jenny thrust a pen at him. "I prayed on this. I fasted on this. I can't do it anymore. I want you gone by the time I get back."

George's eyes glistened. "Jenny, I don't want to lose you. I'll go to church. I'll go to counseling. I'll do whatever it takes. Please don't leave me. Pride made me do this, Jenny. Pride and selfishness. Please give me another chance."

Jenny's face was stone. "You're right. Pride made you lose your wife."

George fell to his knees, tears streaming down his face. "Please, Jenny. If you leave me, I'll die."

Jenny didn't flinch. "It's over, George. Just sign the papers. My lawyer already has all the recordings. Get yourself a good attorney."

She grabbed her keys from the dresser. "I'll be back to get the signed papers."

She walked out of the room without another word. Johnny moved away from the door to let her pass. "Mom, where are you going?"

Jenny didn't answer. She simply left, tears fell as she closed the front door behind her. The house had never felt so quiet. Pride goeth before destruction, and a haughty spirit before a fall. George sat on the edge of the bed, his hands covering his face. He clung to his pride, and in doing so, lost the very gift God had placed in his life. Jenny's love could no longer carry the weight of betrayal. Tonight, the Jenkins' home was shattered by the silence of a love that could endure no more.

Chapter 15

Knowing that Jenny was coming, Pastor Jamal Floyd and First Lady Joyce Floyd prepared their hearts. They were ready, waiting for Jenny when she called while sitting in her car outside. When she stepped through the door, Joyce wrapped Jenny in her arms, holding her like a daughter. Pastor Floyd joined, he embraced them both before gently leading Jenny inside.

"Take her into the study," he said softly. First Lady Floyd guided Jenny to the couch, where Jenny collapsed and sobbed.

"Let it out, Jenny," Joyce whispered. The woman rocked her friend gently. "Crying is good for the soul."

Jenny clung to Joyce, her tears soaking the first lady's blouse, "Lord, please help me! Please, Jesus, help me!" she cried.

"Lord, I don't know what to do. I feel like I'm dying inside. I have no hope left. No strength left."

Jamal quietly poured a glass of water and handed it to his wife. Joyce pressed it into Jenny's hands.

"Drink, sweetheart," she said softly.

Jenny took a small sip, then shook her head. Tears still streamed down her face as she spoke.

"My life is a mess," she whispered. "And I don't know how to fix it."

Joyce gently shook her head. "That's the problem, Jenny. You've been trying to fix it all by yourself. You can't fix this on your own. You have to surrender it, all of it! Let the Lord carry what you can't."

Pastor Floyd nodded, his voice calm and steady. "She's right, Sister Jenny. Learning how to surrender to God will be your first step toward healing."

Jenny looked up, desperate. "But how? How do I surrender? By fasting? By praying more?"

Pastor Floyd placed a reassuring hand on Joyce's shoulder. "Honey, why don't you share your FULL testimony?"

Joyce gave Jenny a small smile. "Our testimony," she corrected gently. "You and the congregation know part of our testimony, but not the full details."

Jenny frowned. "You and Pastor Floyd? What do you mean?"

First Lady Floyd nodded, sitting a little straighter. "Yes, Jenny. Me and Pastor Floyd. Our marriage has been through the fire...and I mean fire."

Jenny blinked, surprised. "You two?"

"Yes," Jamal said quietly. "Us."

Joyce took a deep breath. "When I first met Pastor Floyd, I wasn't a First Lady. I wasn't even saved. I was a broken young woman doing whatever I had to do to survive."

Jenny's eyes widened, her breath catching in her throat. She had never imagined First Lady Floyd, an elegant, wise, and so full of grace carrying a past like that. Jenny leaned forward, unable to hide her shock. She listened while her tear-stained face filled with curiosity.

"You?" she whispered, almost afraid to speak louder, as though the truth might shatter the image she'd always held of Joyce.

Joyce nodded slowly, "Yes, Jenny. Me. My story didn't start in the church. It started on the streets. I was a prostitute. I was angry, bitter, and lost. Jamal had just graduated from college. He was a church boy. He was still a virgin and didn't know much about the streets. One night, he got lost on his way to a revival service.

"When he pulled over and asked me for directions, I thought he was my next client. I asked him how much he'd pay me for the answer."

Jenny's mouth dropped open.

"He laughed," Joyce said, smiling faintly at the memory. "I got angry, thinking he was making fun of me. I snapped at him. And then he said something that changed my life. He said I was 'too beautiful to be standing on that corner.' You don't belong here, he told me."

Her voice softened, almost breaking. "No one had ever said anything like that to me before, Jenny. Not a single person. He didn't see what I was. Jamal saw who I could be." First Lady Floyd smiled softly at Jenny as she continued.

"I said, 'Look dude, do you want the directions or not? If not, keep it moving. I have to make rent.' Jamal just laughed again. I was getting mad. What's so funny? I asked. He smiled and said, The Lord. I rolled my eyes. I was irritated, so I had to ask. What does the Lord have to do with directions? And what's so funny about God? Do you know, Pastor Floyd grinned and said, The Lord and the fact that I never get lost. Yet, here I am standing talking to you."

Jenny gave a little laugh. "Wait, he just said the Lord like that? I would have thought he was crazy too.

Joyce nodded, "Exactly. I shot back at him finally easing up. Well, I have information you're unaware of. I said back to Jamal. Oh really? What's that, young lady? He asked. I smirked. The directions to the church."

Jenny burst into laughter tickling Joyce.

"Jamal burst out laughing too when I said it. You sure do laugh a lot, I said to him remembering that I needed to get back to work. I reminded him I had to make my rent. That's when Pastor Floyd got out of his car and started walking toward me. I pulled out my blade, thinking, Here we go. Another crazy one. But instead of coming at me, he reached into his pocket. How much is your rent? he asked, pulling out a stack of money. I was speechless."

Jenny leaned in, eager now. "Did you take the money?"

"No, not at first," First Lady Floyd said, shaking her head. "At first, I thought he was the police. I didn't know what to do. I just stood there staring at him."

Jamal chuckled at the memory. "So I asked again, "How much is your rent? And why are you out here, really? You don't look like someone hooked on drugs."

"I told him he was wrong," First Lady Floyd said quietly. "I was using, not heavy, but I did cocaine sometimes. I drank a lot. I questioned him about helping me. How do you know I won't take this money and just get high with it?"

Pastor Floyd laughed. "You won't," he said.

"I cracked a joke and asked him, 'Did the Lord tell you that? Then the Lord should have given you the directions to the church!' I burst out laughing again, and Pastor Floyd leaned over to plant a kiss on my cheek. For the first time in my life, I felt safe and could not explain the calmness that came over me. He was different. He never once asked me for anything in return. His spirit was soft.

"So, how much is your rent, Jamal asked again. And do not worry about me being lost. The steps of a good man are ordered.

Pastor Floyd placed his hand on top of First Lady Floyd's hand and smiled at her. He began to speak with such admiration for his wife. "I was so amazed at how beautiful she was. The moonlight was shining on her face, but you couldn't tell me it wasn't the glory of God gleaming on her beautiful brown skin. She was a short, sassy woman, and I have to admit, I was immediately turned on by this. Joyce wasn't someone I would normally be attracted to, but there was something about her and the way she moved. I could feel the softness of her breath on my face. She smelled like strawberries and pineapples. She did not ask me for money or ask if I needed to have sex with her for money. I knew she was different. I wanted her."

"How many hookers do you pick up with these lines?" I asked him. "I was wondering why I wouldn't take the money like any other time. Normally I'd go through hell and high water for rent money. Before I knew it, I blurted out, my rent is seven hundred dollars.

Jamal added to the story and said, "I counted out seven hundred dollars and placed it in her hand."

"I just stood there with my mouth wide open," Joyce said. "I asked him if he was sure the Lord told him to give me the money."

"Yes, He did," Jamal cut into Joyce's story. "And that's not all He told me."

Jenny leaned forward, excited. She never knew this part of their story in such detail. "Really? What else did he say?"

Jamal smiled as he remembered. "I got back into my car, rolled down the passenger-side window, and leaned across the seat. I told her the Lord said you are my wife. I will marry you. Then I pulled off."

"I yelled after his car," Joyce said, laughing softly at the memory. "I thought, now I know you are crazy! And then I cried."

"Yes," Jamal said, "I knew she was my wife. The Lord had shown me in a dream. But as I was driving off that night, I realized something else…"

"What was that?" Jenny asked.

"She never gave me directions to the church."

Jenny laughed. "So how did you get there?"

"I didn't," Pastor Floyd admitted. "I went back home. I fell on my knees as soon as I got there and said, Lord, you've got to be kidding me. A hooker? A prostitute of all people? I wrestled with God all night, but by the morning I knew she was the one He ordained for me."

"Oh, this is such a beautiful love story," Jenny whispered, tears in her eyes.

"This is all the pleasant stuff, Jenny," Lady Floyd said, turning to her. "But there's more to the story. It wasn't always easy."

"No, not easy at all," Jamal added. "I went looking for Joyce every day, but I couldn't find her. I drove around for hours. I didn't even get her name that night, so I couldn't ask anyone. I was so discouraged and I started questioning God. Word got back to my parents that I was hanging around the strip, and eventually I gave up and stopped looking."

Jenny turned to Joyce. "What happened to you? Why couldn't he find you?"

Joyce's face grew somber. "After Jamal pulled off that night, I just stood there staring in the direction of his car in disbelief. I thought maybe I was dreaming. Maybe the cocaine I sniffed earlier had been laced with something. And then suddenly everything went black. Someone shot me three times and robbed me. They shot me once in the stomach, once in the chest, and once in the head. I didn't wake up until weeks later in the hospital."

Jenny gasped. "You were shot?"

Jamal responded to Jenny's question. "I thought I had scared her off for good. I felt like I'd missed God completely. I was so confused. Then one day I was reading the newspaper and saw her picture. It was an update about the shooting. The police caught the men responsible. I dropped the paper and went straight to the hospital."

First Lady Floyd continued, "The person responsible was my ex-husband and his brother. When the police came to arrest them, my ex-brother-in-law gave himself up. My ex-husband shot himself and committed suicide."

Jenny put a hand over her mouth, stunned. "My God."

"What happened when you saw her, Pastor Floyd?" Jenny asked.

"She didn't know who I was. She didn't even know who she was," Pastor Floyd said sadly.

First Lady Floyd nodded. "I had no memory of anything. My aunt and uncle were there. Jamal explained to them how we met that night. My aunt was loving, but I wasn't close to my uncle or cousin. I never wanted to be."

Jenny frowned. "Why? What happened?"

First Lady Floyd's face hardened. "Because my cousin molested me for years. And my uncle...he sexually abused me too. When I woke up, it was like I was back at fourteen again, reliving it. I hadn't told my aunt yet. I loved her, but she had no idea that her husband was the monster he was. He was later arrested for molesting a young girl. That's when my aunt came to me and asked me if he had ever touched me. She learned later that he had also abused their son. My cousin molested me because he was trying to prove he wasn't gay. He committed suicide in prison."

Jenny sat frozen, tears running down her face. "You've been through so much, First Lady."

"The day she woke up," Pastor Floyd said gently, "was the day my journey and her journey of healing and deliverance began."

Jenny's voice cracked as tears welled up. She couldn't believe what she was hearing from First Lady Floyd. But, she wasn't shocked. She had lived that same horror in her own house, growing up.

"My father raped me day and night," she cried. "He was one of the elders at our church. I got pregnant by my dad when I was thirteen. He made me get an abortion in secret. After that, he would use condoms. He made me put them on."

Jenny's words came faster now, each one tearing out of her chest. "I was trapped in that house of horror. Every time I threatened to tell, he would beat my mother and make me watch. He told me he would kill her if I ever said anything. So, to protect my mother, I stayed silent." Jenny's body gave way, and she fell to the floor, sobbing uncontrollably.

"Jenny! Jenny!" Joyce dropped down and wrapped her arms around her, holding her close, rocking her like a child as Jenny's cries shook the room.

"Wow, Jenny." Joyce said. "I knew it. I knew you were violated. The spirit still hoovers over you. The evidence of it is still there. I can smell it."

Jenny wiped her face. Feeling uncomfortable, she looked at Joyce trying to change the subject. "How did you wind back up with the pastor after all this, after you left the hospital?"

"I can finish my story at a later time, the timing of the Lord is right now and the window of deliverance is presenting itself. I don't want to miss it. It's about you, Jenny. Let's talk about you. Your surrendering is happening right now."

Joyce took Jenny's face between her hands. "It's not your fault, Jenny. What happened to you as a child was not your fault. You were a victim, and now you have become victorious. If you can promise me, you will always remain honest, we will get you through this. Stick with me and the Lord and deliverance will come forth".

Jenny shook her head agreeing to stick with Joyce as she processed the First Lady's words.

"Promise me Jenny, that you will stick with me all the way."

"I promise because I want to be free."

"Do not make any decision concerning your marriage just yet." Joyce ordered Jenny in love. " Wait 90 days. 90 days ok. Then after that, we can revisit."

Jenny turned to Joyce. The room itself had grown smaller. She wanted to promise, but the words felt heavy, stuck in her throat. Remembering her past was like ripping open stitches that had barely begun to heal. Images of her father, the pain he caused, the secrets she was forced to keep, and the brokenness of her family all came rushing back like a flood.

Her hands clenched in her lap, "Joyce, I don't know if I can do this. Every time I think about everything I've endured…what my father did, the pain, the lies. It feels like I'm bleeding all over again. I want deliverance…I really do. Hearing your story gave me hope. But this rage inside me, it's so loud right now."

Joyce steadying her gaze on Jenny, spoke sternly. "That rage is why you need to wait, Jenny. Let God do the healing work in these 90 days. This isn't just about George. This is about setting you free from everything that tried to break you."

Jenny took a deep, shaky breath. "Okay," she said finally, her voice barely above a whisper. "I'll try…I'll wait."

Chapter 16

Paula sat curled on the edge of Rick's couch, her arms crossed.

"You know my father is an asshole," she said bitterly. "The way he treats my mother...like crap."

Rick exhaled heavily and nodded. "I know. I've told your dad that before. And listen, I'm not innocent. But your mother? She's a good woman. She doesn't deserve any of this."

Paula looked away, her voice dropping. "She's been through so much. I saw the hurt in her face tonight. But I don't want to talk about that right now." She slid closer to him and kissed his neck, her hand slipping under his shirt. Rick grabbed her wrist gently and pushed her back.

"I called you here for a reason, Paula," he said quietly.

Paula froze and watched him carefully. Every time Rick said those words, he tried to end things. If Steve hadn't been busy,

Paula wouldn't even be there. She was still thinking about her mom. The last thing she wanted was Rick's drama.

"And what reason is that, Rick?" she asked, her tone sharp.

He swallowed hard. "I'm ending this. For real this time. I can't keep doing this. You're too young for me. You're like a niece to me. And your dad, if he ever finds out..."

"My dad?" Paula snapped.

"Yes. Your dad," Rick said firmly. "He's like a brother to me. And now I'm sleeping with his daughter. It's wrong. I feel like a pervert. Paula, you're sixteen. This isn't right."

Paula's jaw clenched. "He doesn't deserve your loyalty. My father is a cheater and a liar who only cares about himself."

"Asshole or not, he's still my best friend," Rick said quietly, rubbing his forehead. "You feel like this now, but your father has been loyal to you too. Out of everyone, he's supported and protected you your whole life. He'd kill for you, Paula. He'd move mountains for you. Yes, he's been a horrible husband. But, he's been a great dad and a true friend to me."

Paula grew angry. "He's been a horrible husband. There's no argument there. So, you want to end this, right? Fine. Whatever. If this is goodbye, then give it to me one last time. I promise I won't reach out to you after tonight."

"No, Paula," Rick said firmly, shaking his head. "I can't."

Paula leaned closer, her lips brushed Rick's neck as she whispered, "Just one more time."

Rick felt her warm breath against his skin and fought to stay firm. "I'm serious this time."

She ignored his protest and slid onto his lap. She could feel his body react beneath her.

"No, Paula."

She smirked and pressed herself closer, making it harder for him to resist. Her perfume filled his senses. She knew exactly what she was doing.

"If you didn't want me to come over here for this, then why are you sitting here in pajama bottoms with no underwear on?" she teased.

She reached down toward him, but he grabbed her hand before she could touch him.

"You are such a Jezebel," he said through gritted teeth. "You're too young."

Paula unbuttoned her blouse slowly, her eyes locked on his.

"Then send me home if you don't want me," she said softly. "Just say it. Tell me you don't want me anymore."

Rick turned his head away, but she reached for him again, refusing to let go.

"I don't want you anymore," Rick said, lying through his teeth. He was trying to fight the feeling, but his body was betraying him. His heart said no, his penis was going against the plan and saying something else.

Paula smirked, hearing the quickness of his breath. "Then why are you breathing so hard?" she whispered, pressing her wet lips against his neck. "Just one more time, Rick. I promise I'll leave you alone."

Rick closed his eyes, fighting himself. "Just one more time," he murmured, already caving. "I mean it, Paula. This is the last time."

Paula laughed softly, a dangerous little laugh that let Rick know she had him exactly where she wanted him. "Yeah," she said with a wicked grin. "I hear you."

The house was quiet as Jenny stepped inside. The woman closed the door softly behind her. The silence felt heavy, almost sacred, but it didn't bring her peace. She walked down the hall and peeked into Paula's room, empty. Jenny opened John John's door. He wasn't there either.

She stood in the hallway, gripping the doorframe. She wanted to call them out, to hear their voices, but she wasn't ready to face George. Not yet. First Lady Floyd's words echoed in her mind: "Don't decide until ninety days."

"Ninety days...three whole months," she whispered. "Lord, how am I supposed to wait that long? How do I live in this house another day, let alone three months?"

Jenny sank onto the couch and buried her face in her hands, her tears spilled hot down her face. "Lord, I need you right now," she cried.

"Fill me up again. I can't do this without You. I miss worshiping You, God! Please...speak to me. Please give me fresh oil, give me strength!" A gentle hand touched her shoulder. Jenny flinched, startled, then looked up through blurry tears. It was Juanita.

Jenny's mother-in-law sat beside her without a word, gathering Jenny into her arms. And there, on that couch, both women wept together. They cried for the pain they had endured and for the broken pieces of their family.

Jenny and Juanita finally broke their embrace to talk. "It's late, Momma. Why are you here?"

"George called me," Juanita said softly. "He told me everything."

Jenny froze. "George?"

"Yes," Juanita nodded, her expression heavy. "He called me crying...yelling, too."

Jenny frowned. "Why would he take his anger out on you?"

"He's not, baby," Juanita said, reaching for her hand. "He's scared. Scared to death. He doesn't want you to divorce him."

Jenny pulled back, her voice sharp. "He's scared because he's afraid I'll take him for everything. That's all, Mom. He's afraid to lose what he's built, not afraid to lose me."

Juanita shook her head slowly. "No, Jenny. That's not all it is."

Jenny's eyes burned as she stood, pacing. "Mom, I heard him with that woman, with Rick, with people in his office. He jokes about me. Cruel jokes. Do you know what that feels like? To hear the man you love mock you like you're nothing?"

Juanita's heart ached as she listened. "That was all pride talking, Jenny. A man's pride."

Jenny stopped pacing, her tears falling freely now. "Pride that cost him his marriage. I can't do this any longer." She turned and looked her mother-in-law in the eye. Juanita reached to grab her daughter-in-law's hands.

"Why would you even want me to stay with George, Mom? Why?"

Juanita said nothing, so Jenny pressed harder. "I know he's your son. I know you love him. But if I were your daughter, your actual daughter, would you want me to make the same mistakes you made?"

Juanita let go of Jenny's hands and sighed deeply.

"No disrespect, Mom," Jenny said, her voice breaking, "you know how much I love you. But if I was your blood daughter, would you really want me to stay with George? Or would you help me pack his bags?"

Juanita's eyes softened with pain. "Jenny, no…it's not that I want you to stay in this mess. If you were my daughter, yes…I would help you pack his bags myself." She took Jenny's hand again, squeezing it.

"But, George is my son. And I've seen, in the twenty-five years you've been together, how you've brought the best out of him. Jenny, I know my son loves you. If only he could get past all this anger and hurt inside him."

Jenny shook her head, tears streaming down her face. "It feels like all I pull out of him is hate. What about the pain he's caused me, Mom? The nights I cried myself to sleep, the STD he brought home, the pregnancy with this woman?"

Juanita caught her breath violently. "How...how do you know about the other woman?"

Jenny's expression hardened. "I have a video, Mom. Audio recordings of their conversations. I know everything. And I know you knew."

Juanita closed her eyes, guilt washing over her face. "I'm sorry, Jenny. I really am. I just...I didn't want you to leave him. I didn't want to hurt you, that's why I helped him."

Jenny's voice rose, anger finally breaking through the grief. "No, you helped him because he's your son. And you've always taken up for him. You know what? I keep hearing the same thing over and over: I didn't want to hurt you. John John blackmails his father because he didn't want to hurt me. Paula keeps quiet so she doesn't lose her cash flow. George...George says he didn't mean to hurt me. And now you, Mom. You helped this woman get an abortion, but you also 'didn't want to hurt me.'"

Jenny's shoulders shook as she looked at her mother-in-law, betrayed. "Wow. All of you made decisions for me. You chose not because you cared about my pain, but because you didn't want to face the truth yourselves."

Juanita's own tears fell without any reservations. She reached for Jenny's face and held it gently. "I really didn't want to hurt you. I love you, Jenny. You are my daughter; maybe not by blood, but by heart. And no matter what happens between you and George, that will never change."

Jenny's voice cracked, her sobs came harder as years of pain poured out.

"Everybody has a funny way of showing me how much they love me!" she cried. "My mother, my father, my uncle, my cousins, my husband, my daughter, my son…and now you, my mother-in-law! And let's not forget my brother!"

Her hands shook as she clutched at her chest. "All of y'all claim you love me, but all you've ever done is hurt me! Hurt me over and over again! I am tired, Mom…I'm so tired of hurting. I can't take it anymore!"

Her voice dropped to a whisper, her words trembling like fragile glass. "I'd rather die than keep feeling like this. I've been hurting my whole life. When does it stop? When will someone love me for real?"

Tears streamed down her face as she collapsed onto the couch, rocking back and forth. "I'm a failure. My oldest son is sitting in prison. GT is all messed up because of me! I'm a horrible mother, a horrible wife, a horrible daughter…"

Her voice cracked again. "I'm just…a horrible person."

Jenny collapsed to the floor, curling into a knot, rocking back and forth as she cried. "I just want to die," she sobbed.

"The Lord doesn't love me anymore. That's why He took my worship away. He doesn't love me anymore. My only safe place is gone. I have nothing left."

Her cries grew louder, raw and uncontrollable. Juanita dropped to her knees and wept alongside her all over again.

"Lord, what do I do?" Juanita cries out. "How can I help her?"

Juanita stood up quickly, wiping her tears. She went to the kitchen to grab her phone and call the Floyds. When Jaunita returned, the living room was empty.

"Jenny?!" Juanita called out, panic rising in her chest. She ran down the hall and found the bedroom door locked.

"Jenny! Please, honey, open the door for me. Please!"

Inside, Jenny's voice came through, broken and distant. "I don't want to live anymore. Please just leave me alone."

Juanita leaned against the door, tears streaming.

"Go away! Just let me be," Jenny sobbed.

"I can't do that, baby. You're scaring me. Please, just open the door for me. I promise, I'll leave you alone if you want. But, just let me see you."

Jenny's crying became louder. She let out ugly, heart-wrenching cries. "Please, Lord," she screamed through the sobs.

"Help me!"

Juanita's voice cracked as she banged on the door with her fists. "Don't say that, Jenny! Please, honey, open the door!" She threw her weight against the door, trying to push it open, but it didn't budge.

"Jenny, please...please open the door, baby," Juanita pleaded.

"I don't want to hurt anymore. Please, please help me, Lord. My heart hurts, my soul hurts. Please help me! Please help me!" Jenny screamed over and over again.

"Open the door, Jenny. We will help you!" Juanita's own voice cracked as tears streamed down her face. "Lord Jesus, hear my cry right now. Please, Lord, cover Jenny. Cover her right now!"

The front door opened suddenly.

"Mom? What's going on?" George rushed inside, his face full of concern.

"Oh, my George!" Juanita collapsed into his arms. She shook with emotion

"What's happening?" George asked, panicked.

"It's Jenny. She's locked herself in the bedroom. She was crying uncontrollably, saying she doesn't want to live anymore. George, I've never seen Jenny like this." Juanita's voice broke.

"I have an eerie feeling. I feel the spirit of death in this house."

George's heart pounded as he ran to the bedroom door. "Jenny, open the door, honey! Please open the door!" There was silence. Then, faintly, he heard her crying.

"Please, Jenny. Please open the door."

"I'm tired," her voice finally came through, broken and low. "I'm tired..."

A gunshot shattered the air.

"NO!" George kicked the door open with all his strength. Jenny lay slumped on the floor, a Bible clutched in one hand and a gun in the other. Tears still streaked her face.

Juanita screamed. George dropped to his knees, cradling Jenny's head in his arms.

"Jenny! Jenny, why? Why would you do this?" Juanita ran to call 911 as George rocked Jenny in his arms.

"Please, Lord, no! Please, Lord!" George sobbed.

Jenny's lips trembled as she whispered, "Because I'm tired…"

She took one last breath and went limp.

George screamed, his cries echoing through the house as he clutched Jenny's lifeless body. "No, Lord! No, Lord! Jenny, please! Please don't leave me, Jenny! Mom! Mom! Mom!"

Chapter 17

George paced the hospital hallway, his body trembling as if the floor beneath him might give way.

"This has to be a dream," he muttered to himself, his hands clutched his head. "Yes, that's it. I'm dreaming. My wife didn't do this to me. Jenny is fine. She's still here with me, we're working on our marriage. Any second now, I'll wake up."

His thoughts were interrupted by a gentle touch on his shoulders. Pastor Jamal Floyd and his wife Lady Joyce Floyd stood before him.

"Brother George," Jamal said softly.

George stared straight ahead, his eyes hollow. He didn't speak. Joyce wiped her tears. She had been on the phone with Jenny when she heard the gunshot and then George's scream. She quietly prayed under her breath as her hands trembled.

Down the hall, Juanita was still on the phone with John John, who was yelling through the receiver.

"Just come to the hospital, John John," Juanita urged, her voice shaking. "Try calling your sister. I can't reach her."

Jaunita hung up and turned to see her son standing motionless, staring into nothing. She walked over and wrapped her arms around him. George let out a gut-wrenching scream as Juanita held him.

"What did I do?" George cried, his voice breaking. "What did I do to her? I did this to her. This is my fault. I killed my wife. I caused her so much pain she...she didn't want to live anymore. It's my fault, Lord! It's my fault!"

He fell to his knees right there in the hallway, sobbing. Pastor Floyd knelt down beside him, placing his hand gently on George's head.

"Brother George," Jamal said, his voice steady but full of compassion. "Will you pray with me for Jenny?"

George looked up at him, conflicted. Normally, George didn't care for Jamal. He never had. He had resented Jenny's closeness with the Floyds. George was jealous of how she turned to them when she wouldn't turn to him. But right now? None of that mattered. George lowered his head. He didn't move Jamal's hand away.

"If it's for Jenny," he whispered, "then yes. Pray."

At this point, George didn't care about anything...not his business, not his pride, not even his anger. The only thing that mattered was Jenny and why he hadn't heard a word about her condition.

"I don't want to pray," George muttered, "but you can." He buried his face in his hands and began sobbing silently as if agreeing with himself to let someone else do what he couldn't.

Jamal and Joyce prayed aloud, "Dear Heavenly Father, we come before You tonight, asking You for another dose of mercy. Lord, we know we don't deserve it. But because You love us, we ask You. Surround Jenny right now with Your power. Seat her in a hedge of protection. Death, you have no authority here. We rebuke you in the mighty name of Jesus and call LIFE to overtake you! Lord, we speak life over Jenny's body. We pray for full recovery. Cover Brother George right now. You know his heart even when we don't. Cover him with Your precious blood. In Jesus' name, we seal this prayer. Amen."

Just as they finished praying, the doors to the operating room opened. "Mr. Jenkins?" the doctor said, stepping toward them.

George leapt to his feet. "Yes, Doctor?" His voice cracked.

"Hi, I'm Dr. Ross," the doctor said gently.

George's heart pounded. "Is my wife okay? Is she still alive?"

Juanita grabbed George's arm, her eyes wide with terror.

"Please, Doctor," she begged. "Don't tell me she's gone. Please don't say that!"

George's chest tightened as he whispered, "Doctor...you're not saying she's dead, right?" He collapsed back into the chair, bracing himself for the worst.

Dr. Ross shook his head. "No, I'm not saying that. But she is barely holding on. Your wife is in critical condition. The bullet missed all major organs and is lodged in her back. She is stable for now, but the next 24 hours will be critical."

Juanita covered her face and wept. George bowed his head, whispering, "Thank You, Lord," through tears.

First Lady Floyd wiped her tears and asked softly, "Doctor, if the bullet missed all major organs, why is she barely holding on?"

The doctor looked at her, then extended his hand. "And your name?"

George spoke up before First Lady Floyd could answer. "This is my mother, and this is our pastor and his wife, Pastor and First Lady Floyd."

The doctor nodded solemnly. "Yes, she is stable, but still critical. And there is something else that concerns us even more."

George's stomach dropped. "Something else? What do you mean?"

The doctor took a deep breath. "In the process of removing the bullet — which, thankfully, missed her spinal cord. We found a mass in the center of her abdomen."

George blinked. "A mass?"

"A tumor," the doctor clarified gently. "Roughly the size of a large grapefruit."

George felt the room tilt. "What? A tumor?"

"Yes," the doctor said, his tone grave. "I've seen this type of tumor before."

George's voice trembled. "Is it cancer, Doc?"

The doctor hesitated. "Mr. Jenkins, I dislike giving you a definitive answer until the lab results come back. We took a biopsy and sent it for testing."

Juanita stepped forward, tears welling. "But you said you've seen this before...is it cancerous?"

The doctor's eyes softened. "Yes. I am fairly certain it's cancer. But we won't be absolutely sure until we get the pathology report back."

"Cancer..." Juanita whispered. Joyce gasped and covered her mouth. Jamal wrapped his arm around her.

George's knees nearly buckled. "You're telling me my wife might have cancer? Doctor, please tell me that's not what you're saying. Please don't tell me that..."

"Mr. Jenkins," the doctor said gently, "your wife is very sick. Right now, our priority is keeping her alive through the night. She has a long, hard journey ahead of her."

Juanita wiped her tears angrily. "If you had her open already, why didn't you remove the tumor? Why leave it there?"

George shook his head, frustrated. "Yes, why didn't you just take it out?"

"It's not that simple," the doctor explained. "Given her weakened state from blood loss and trauma, removing the tumor would have been too dangerous. She would not have survived the surgery. We need to get her stable before we can talk about removing it."

The room went silent until Johnny's voice cut through like a knife.

"What the hell did you do to my mom?!" Johnny shouted, stepping around the Floyds.

"Johnny!" Juanita tried to grab him, but he shook her off.

"Did you shoot my mother?!" Johnny's voice broke with rage. He turned to the doctor. "Tell me the truth, because I know my mother would never shoot herself. Not unless something pushed her that far. And I know exactly who pushed her!" He pointed at George.

Juanita stepped between them. "John John, no! Your father didn't shoot her. Your mother…she shot herself."

Johnny's face twisted with anger. "You're lying! You've always covered for him! You always take his side!"

"Johnny," Juanita said softly, tears streaming. "You're upset right now, and I understand that. So I'm going to let this slide."

George, who had been silent, stood up and marched toward Johnny, his fist balled at his side.

"Boy," George growled, his voice low and dangerous, "don't you ever disrespect my mother again. Do you hear me? Never speak to my mother like that…not ever. Do I make myself clear?"

Johnny glared at George, his voice rising. "Now ain't that the kettle calling the pot black. You disrespect my mother every day. But, now you care? You made her shoot herself! I hope you're happy. Maybe she dies. Isn't that what you want? So you can run off with your whore. I hate you!"

Paula and Rick came running down the hallway. "Daddy! Daddy, where's my mom? What's going on?" Paula cried.

Johnny turned to her, his eyes wild. "He killed her! The bastard killed her! Mommy would never do this to herself. She's not that weak. He did something. I know he did!"

Paula's knees buckled. She fainted, and Rick caught her before she hit the floor. George stormed forward to take her from Rick's arms, shooting Rick a deadly glare. Before he could grab her, Johnny pulled Paula away.

"Don't you touch my sister!" Johnny shouted. "You might kill her like you did my mother. Matter of fact, where is she? Why can't we see her?"

Juanita stepped forward sharply. "That's enough, John John! Your father did not kill your mother. She is alive. Instead of attacking your father, you should be praying for your mother's recovery!"

Joyce nodded in agreement. "She's right. Stop speaking death over your mother and speak life. She is still here."

Johnny's voice cracked. "Barely. And I still don't believe you. My mother would never shoot herself. I wish you all would stop saying that!"

Joyce stepped close, placing her hand gently on the young boy's back. "Johnny...she did. I was on the phone with her. I heard the shot. But, listen to me. She's not dead. She still has life, and you have the authority to speak life over her. Don't give up on her."

Johnny broke down sobbing. George took Paula from her brother's arms. She stirred awake and, seeing her father, immediately pulled away.

"Where's my mom?" Paula demanded, her voice shaking. "Where is she? Did John John say you killed her? You selfish, heartless, cheating bastard! You couldn't just let her leave, could you? Jesus, please. Where is my mother? I want to see my mother!"

Juanita suddenly slapped Paula across the face. "Watch your mouth, young lady! How dare you speak to your father like that. Your mother taught you better."

Johnny stepped forward, fists clenched. "Taking up for your son again, Grandma? Did you slap him for cheating on my mother? For mistreating her? For knocking up another woman?"

George's face turned red. He lunged at Johnny, grabbing him by the collar and pulling him close. "You can say whatever you want to me, boy. But you will respect my mother. Do I make myself clear?"

Johnny glared back but didn't resist. "Crystal," he spat.

George released him. Juanita wrapped her arms around Paula, whispering, "Your mother is still alive. Don't listen to Johnny. She's alive."

Johnny muttered bitterly, "Barely...thanks to him."

Paula wiped her tears, looking between them all. "My mom...can I see her, Daddy? Please? I just want to see her." She collapsed into her father's chest.

George's own tears fell as he held Paula. Somehow through all that commotion the doctor was still present. "Doctor, please, can we see her?"

The doctor shook his head. "Not right now. I suggest you all take some time to calm yourselves. Mrs. Jenkins does not need this kind of stress. She is very fragile. Any stress could be too much for her right now."

The doctor's voice softened as he looked at George. "Your wife had to be in a very dark, very depressed place to take a step to end her own life, Mr. Jenkins. That's another issue we will have to address as well. Her healing is not just her physical recovery, but her emotional and mental well-being."

The words hit George like a punch. Paula and Johnny both turned away, struggling to take it in.

Paula blinked. "Wait...what do you mean? Take her own life? Are you saying my mother tried to kill herself?"

Juanita touched her granddaughter's face. "Yes, baby. She shot herself."

Paula's eyes filled with disbelief. "She...she shot herself? My mother? She tried to kill herself?"

Johnny clenched his fists. "Yes. That's what they're telling us."

Paula's voice cracked as she stumbled back a step. "Why? Why? Why would she do that?"

Johnny's anger flared, his words sharp enough to cut the air between them. "Really, Paula? You're looking at the reason. He's standing right in front of you!"

George broke down then, sobs shaking his shoulders. Juanita wrapped her arms around him, holding her son as though she could somehow shield him from the pain. Johnny looked at his father for a long moment, the sight of George's tears rattling him more than he expected. He turned to walk away but stopped. He was torn between rage and pity. He realized while his mother was fighting for her life in one room, his father was breaking apart in this one.

The doctor stepped forward, his voice calm but firm. "For the next hour, I will allow two visitors at a time. Ten minutes each, no more," he said, placing a steadying hand on George's arm. "Mr. Jenkins, it will take a few days for the lab work to return. When it does, we will discuss the other issue."

Paula's head snapped toward him. "Other issues? What other issue?" she demanded, her wide eyes darting between the doctor and her father. "Daddy, what is he talking about? What other issue?"

George opened his mouth but said nothing, the weight of the moment silencing him.

"Thank you, Doctor," Jamal said quietly, stepping forward to shake the man's hand. The doctor gave a final nod before walking away down the hall.

Joyce's composure finally broke. She turned into her husband's chest and wept as Jamal wrapped his arms around her, holding her close and whispering prayers under his breath. The pastor asked God to cover Jenny and strengthen the family for the days ahead. George broke down again. This time Paula was the one to come to his side. He put his face in his hands as sobs shook his shoulders. Johnny turned glanced back and saw the raw grief on his father's face. For the first time, anger slipped into something else. Johnny was struck with confusion and compassion. He walked down the hallway, needing space.

Just as Johnny tried to get some air, two detectives appeared at the end of the hallway. Their presence was sharp, cutting through the already heavy air. One of them, a tall man with a shaved head, flashed his badge.

"Mr. Jenkins?" he asked, his tone formal but not unkind.

George straightened, still holding Paula against him. "Yes, I'm George Jenkins."

"I'm Detective Brown, and this is my partner, Detective Windbush," the man said, nodding toward the woman beside him. "We know this is not a good time, but we do need to ask you a few questions about what happened tonight."

Juanita stiffened and moved closer to her son. "Detectives, she shot herself. I was there. I heard her crying through the door. George was banging on it, begging her to open it. She...she wouldn't."

"It's true. I was on the phone as well. I heard it all." Joyce shuddered at the remembrance.

Detective Windbush took out a small notepad. "Ma'am, we understand, and we're very sorry for what your family is going through. But since there was a firearm involved and your wife is now in critical condition, we are required to take a statement from everyone who was present at the time of the incident."

George swallowed hard, his throat dry. "You think I had something to do with this?" As he responded to the detectives, Paula moved closer to Rick. Somehow she felt safer next to him than by her own father.

"No one's accusing you of anything," Detective Brown said evenly, "but we need a clear timeline of who was in the house, who heard what, and who had access to the firearm. Mr. Jenkins, we'd like all of you all to come down to the station to give formal statements."

"Tonight?" Juanita asked softly.

"As soon as possible," Windbush replied. "We need this on record while it's still fresh in everyone's mind."

George glanced back at the hospital doors where his wife was fighting for her life. He nodded reluctantly. "Fine. I'll go. But as soon as Jenny wakes up, I'm coming right back."

Detective Brown gave him a brief nod. "Understood, Mr. Jenkins. We'll try not to take too long."

Johnny walked up quietly, his face still hot with anger, but softer now as he looked between Paula and their father. "You still think he didn't do it?" he asked under his breath, his voice low but sharp enough for Paula to hear.

Paula didn't answer. She grabbed a hold of Rick's hand tightly, her silence saying everything she couldn't put into words.

The hallway was quiet again, but the tension was deafening. The family was splintered. The love between them had torn between grief, anger, and suspicion. The night was far from over.

Paula stood frozen. "Daddy...you didn't—"

George cut her off gently but firmly. "No, Paula. I didn't. But, since today is all about getting to the truth, I'm going to clear this up so nobody has to wonder."

The detectives stepped aside to let George and Juanita prepare to leave, the weight of their presence lingered in the hall like a storm cloud. The night had already been unbearable, but now a new layer of tension wrapped itself around the Jenkins family. The heaviness followed them out of the hospital and into the unknown.

Chapter 18

The cold, sterile smell of the precinct hit them as soon as they stepped inside. Bleach, old coffee, and the weight of too many confessions surrounded them. The fluorescent lights buzzed overhead. It was too bright and too honest.

George walked ahead. His jaw was tight and one arm draped protectively around Paula's shoulders. Johnny trailed behind. He glared at his father's back like the man himself was the problem. Rick kept space between himself and George. His hands were shoved deep into his pockets and his eyes avoided everyone. Juanita and First Lady Floyd followed silently, as they whispered prayers under their breath.

Detective Brown stepped forward, voice calm and professional. "Thank you for coming in tonight. We know this is difficult, but we need everyone's statements to close this out properly."

George nodded stiffly, "Let's get this over with."

Detective Windbush held up a clipboard and read the group their Miranda Rights. "Before we start, procedure requires that we interview each of you separately."

Paula's head snapped up. Johnny shifted uneasily. Rick froze. One by one, officers guided them away. Johnny went down the hall to Interview Room 2. Paula was directed to the room across from Johnny. Juanita and George were escorted towards Interview Room 1 and 4.

Rick was held in the hallway as a "known associate." His presence was noted but Rick was not questioned yet.

The Jenkins' family was questioned about who was at the house or on the phone and what they heard. The kids had to detail the times of arrival to the house, their whereabouts before coming home and who they were with. Detectives compared every timeline against the others.

Afterwards, the detectives called them all into a larger interview room. They wanted to see if every detail matched. Paula and Johnny were told to wait until they were invited in.

Detective Brown gestured to the table. "Have a seat."

George sat. Juanita lowered into the chair beside him. And First Lady Floyd sat down near Juanita. George's jaw flexed. He hated not being in control. Anger was easier to wear than fear.

Detective Brown flipped open a notebook. "Walk us through the moments leading up to the incident again. Detail times. Who was home?"

George exhaled sharply. "I already told you. Jenny locked herself in the bedroom. She was crying. I begged her to open the door. I heard the shot and kicked the door in. That's it. My mother was there. She can confirm."

Juanita nodded, voice trembling. "Yes. I called Pastor Floyd and First Lady Floyd before it happened. First Lady Floyd stayed on the phone the whole time."

"Good," Brown said, jotting it down. "That supports your timeline."

Detective Brown looked toward the door. "Bring the children in."

Johnny slumped into the seat opposite the detectives with his arms crossed like armor. Paula sat next to him, her leg bounced uncontrollably.

Detective Windbush softened her tone. "Johnny, where were you between 6 and 9 p.m.?"

Johnny glanced at his father, then back at the detective. "At Kent's house. Playing video games. Kent's mom saw me."

Detective Brown evaluated him carefully. "We'll verify that."

Windbush turned to Paula. "And you?"

Paula swallowed. She felt Rick's presence behind her without even looking.

"I was...out with a friend from school. We went to the mall."

"Which friend?" Brown asked.

Paula hesitated. Her stomach twisted. She could feel Rick watching her silently praying she wouldn't crack. If detectives checked everything would blow up.

"Uh...Judy. You can ask her if you want."

First Lady Floyd lifted an eyebrow. She knew Paula was lying but chose to intercede silently instead of attempting to speak.

Brown made another note. "We'll follow up. Standard procedure."

Detective Brown paused his writing and glanced between Juanita and First Lady Floyd.

"First Lady Floyd," he clarified, "you were on the phone at the time of the incident?"

She nodded with steady authority. "Yes. From the moment Juanita called, all the way through the 911 dispatch. I heard everything."

Detective Windbush exchanged a look with Brown. She wasn't skeptical of First Lady Floyd because she recognized her. Everyone in the city knew the Floyds. Pastor Floyd wasn't just a pastor; he sat on community boards, police advisory committees, and half the officers attended his church.

Brown closed his notebook. "That aligns with the emergency call logs," he said.

"Your timeline checks out."

Windbush capped her pen. "At this point, with the corroborated witness and matching statements, there's no legal reason to hold you."

The tension in the room shifted. No one was relieved, but the worry seemed to loosen.

George blinked. "So...we're free to go?"

Brown nodded. "Yes, sir. Given the circumstances, and the credibility of the witness on the phone, we're releasing all of you."

Nobody missed what Brown implied. They were free to leave, because of who vouched for them. When First Lady Floyd spoke, the room listened. George reached for Paula's hand. For the first time that night, she didn't pull away. Johnny shoved his chair back and walked out without looking at his father. They stepped into the cool night air, a stark contrast to the harsh fluorescent interrogation rooms.

Behind them, the precinct doors closed with a metallic thud like a judgment sealing itself. First Lady Floyd looked directly at Rick. Her voice was low but sharp, meant for him to hear.

"The truth always has a way of coming out, sooner or later."

Rick froze for a moment and met her gaze before quickly looking away. Something about her words lingered in the air like smoke. Every word she said was a heavy, prophetic warning. The tension between them was thick enough to cut with a knife. First Lady Floyd's eyes lingered on Rick, then shifted to Paula, as if piecing together a puzzle only she could see. Johnny crossed his arms tightly across his chest, his eyes narrowed on Rick with quiet suspicion.

Rick cleared his throat, shifting uncomfortably under Johnny's stare.

"George," he said cautiously, "are you going back to the hospital tonight? I can head over there if you want...sit with

Jenny, make sure everything's good. Someone should be there in case she wakes up."

Juanita stepped forward, clutching her purse. "If anyone goes, it should be me. Jenny needs family by her side."

George nodded slightly, his voice softer. "Thanks, Mom. I'll rest better knowing you're there."

No one said another word. The dysfunction hung thick in the air as they all exchanged brief, quiet hugs. One by one, they departed into the night. Each of the Jenkins carried their own thoughts, their own secrets, and the heavy weight of what just unfolded.

Chapter 19

The house was still, unnervingly quiet. After the questioning at the station, George, Juanita, and the kids had been released. First Lady Floyd's statement, finalizing that she was on the phone when Jenny shot herself, was the only reason the police let George go.

George stepped into the bedroom slowly, as if the walls themselves might accuse him. The smell of iron still lingered, and his chest tightened as his eyes fell on the dark stain in the carpet where Jenny had collapsed.

He sank to his knees. His tears came hard and fast. Drops fell onto the floor as George crawled to the bathroom closet, grabbed an empty bucket, and filled it with water. He returned and sat cross-legged on the floor, soaking a sponge and trying to scrub the blood away. His hands trembled as he worked.

Jenny's voice echoed in his mind, painfully clear.

"I'm tired, George. I'm tired. I need you to spend some time with me. I miss you, George."

George shook his head, pressing the sponge to the floor harder.

"I love you, George. I want you. Don't you love me anymore?"

His own memory of his voice rang out in response.

"No, Jenny, I don't. I hate you, Jenny."

Her sobs reverberated in his head like ghosts trapped in the room.

George dropped the sponge and clutched his head. "Lord, please help me!" His voice broke into a sob. "Wait a minute. Just, wait a minute...I don't deserve Jenny. This is all my fault. I should be the one in the hospital, not her. Jenny should be here. She's a good woman, and I caused all this pain!"

His hands searched under the bed for the blood he couldn't quite reach and hit something solid.

"What is this?"

George pulled out the DVD, its plastic casing smeared with a faint, bloody handprint. His chest heaved as he stood and walked to the TV. With shaking hands, he slid the disc into the player. Static flickered, then a familiar voice filled the room.

Cassandra's voice echoed "Oh, honey!"

A man's voice followed behind her seductively, "Hey, sweetie. What time did he leave?"

"Not too long ago. Boy, I'm glad. I don't know how much longer I can put up with this."

"Me either. Let's not waste time. I'm horny."

Cassandra replied to the man, "Mmm, come on, sweetie…"

George's jaw clenched. His stomach twisted. It wasn't just any man. George recognized the voice. It was one of his own employees from the trucking company. Jenny had been telling the truth all along.

His heart pounded as the tape continued to play.

George's recorded voice played on the TV, "Hey, Cassandra."

"Hey, Big Daddy. I miss you."

"I miss you too. What have you been up to all day?"

"Nothing. I was here all night and all day, waiting on you."

George shot up from the floor, pointing at the screen. "Liar!" His voice boomed through the room. "Damn slut!"

But the recording kept going, like salt in an open wound.

"Come over here. I feel like pounding on some beef. Been holding myself all day. Jenny wanted me earlier, but I couldn't. All I wanted was to be here. My body's throbbing for Miss Sandy, not Jenny." George listened to his words in shame.

"Don't you want to take a shower first?" Cassandra asked.

"Yeah, I need to take a shower. Don't you want to join?"

George staggered back, disgusted with himself. He slammed his fist against the dresser, the sound echoing in the hollow room.

"God, what have I done?" His voice cracked. His legs gave way, and he collapsed onto the floor, sobbing.

"No honey, I just took a shower. Enjoy yourself. I'll be right here waiting, naked and horny."

The faint sound of running water echoed through the speakers.

Cassandra picked up the phone and called someone. "Hey Vincent, plans change."

The familiar male voice sharply responded. "What do you mean plans change?"

"George is here. The plans have changed."

"Put his ass out. I'm horny."

"How do you sound? How can I put him out of his own apartment? He pays all my bills. I'd put your ass out first before I put him out. He is my meal ticket. If I say plans change, then plans change. You hear me, Vincent?" Cassandra whispered her threat to her other man.

"I hear you, Cassandra. But I'll tell you this, if his ass ain't gone by the morning, I'm coming anyway."

"I gotta go. He's coming. I'll call you once he leaves."

"You better."

The sound of the shower cut off in the distance.

Cassandra's voice returned to a normal volume. "Wow, that was quick."

George's voice on the tape got louder too as he exited the shower still dripping, "I can't stay long. I have to get back home early tonight."

"You know, George, you make me feel like I'm some cheap whore. Is this all you want from me?"

"No, I love you. Don't you know I love you, Sandy? Let me show you how much I love you..."

George gritted his teeth. "You dumb bastard," he muttered to himself, tears streaking his face. "She's been playing you, bro."

He fast-forwarded through more footage, his stomach dropping as he saw Vincent coming and going over the years. There was his proof that Jenny had been right all along. George's phone rang, Cassandra's name flashing on the screen. He answered, his voice cold.

"George! George!" Cassandra's voice was urgent. "Honey, are you there? Answer me, George."

"Look, Cassandra, I'm going through a lot. I'll hit you back later."

"What do you mean you'll call me later?"

"Just what I said. I'll call you later."

"George, I'm tired of this. What is it now? Jenny not feeling good? Her dog died? What's the excuse this time?"

"Look, bitch. Didn't I just tell you I'm going through a lot?"

A pause. "Wait. Did you just call me a bitch?"

George didn't answer.

"I know you just didn't call me a bitch!"

"Yes, I did," he growled. "Slut. Whore. Jezebel. Stop me if I'm wrong. Gold digger. Liar."

"Where is all this coming from?"

"Look, it's over. I want you out in thirty days."

"Out where?"

"Out of my apartment. Out of my life. For good."

"George, wait! Why? What's going on?"

"I'm not playing with you, whore. Get out of my place in thirty days. If you piss me off, you'll be out earlier than that."

"But where am I supposed to go?"

"Ask Luke. Or Vincent. Or maybe you can shack up with your dead-ass mama. I don't care where you go. It's over. I was about to leave my wife for you, but I won't make that mistake. Not anymore."

"What about the baby? What am I supposed to do? Where am I supposed to go?"

George laughed bitterly. "There is no baby. You've been lying to me this whole time. Get your shit and get out."

He hung up before she could respond, throwing the phone onto the bed. "Fucking whore," he muttered, wiping his face.

The room was silent except for the sound of water sloshing in the bucket as he went back to scrubbing the carpet. His phone rang again and again. Cassandra's name flashed each time, but he ignored it.

As he worked, tears fell. Then, gently, Paula knelt beside him. Without saying a word, she took the sponge from his hand and began wiping the blood herself. Father and daughter stayed there on the floor together, crying in silence as they cleaned away what was left of Jenny's pain. Sin leaves a stain deeper than flesh and blood. Sometimes, those left behind are forced to carry the cloth, scrub at the mess and try to wipe away what can never truly be undone.

Chapter 20

Johnny sat on the edge of his bed with his phone pressed to his ear. He filled Kent in on everything that happened. Johnny even included the devastating news that his mother might have had cancer.

"Wow, man," Kent said quietly, letting out a long breath. "That's crazy. Where's your father now?" Johnny stood up, leaned back against the wall as he listened and stared at the ceiling.

"He went to pick up GT from jail. He got released early for good behavior. He was supposed to get out next week, but they let him out a few days early."

Kent whistled softly. "Your brother is coming home today? Man, that's a walking miracle right there. God is really looking out for him."

Johnny gave a short nod. "Yeah…yeah, I know. But he's gonna be pissed."

"Does he even know what happened to your mom?"

"No. Pops was supposed to tell him."

Kent hesitated. "You think he's gonna tell him the whole story?"

Johnny gave a short, bitter laugh. "If I know my father, he won't. He acts like he's not scared of GT, but I see it every time GT's around. My brother's got a lot of anger in him. He can be really violent."

Kent shook his head. "You're right. I still don't know how he only got five years for killing that man. Shot him six times and shot the other man two. And he only did five years. That's wild."

Johnny smirked. "That's Momma. She fasted and prayed the whole time. They called it temporary insanity, but GT meant to kill that man. He just got off easy because of her prayers."

"Yeah, that wasn't self-defense. Six shots?" Kent whistled again. "Man, your mom's prayers must really hit heaven. If I ever get in trouble, I want your mom to pray for me."

Johnny smirked faintly. "Yeah, she prays."

"She gon' be okay," Kent said firmly. "Everything's gonna be fine. Watch and see. And don't just sit there being sad. You know I prayed too, John John."

"You prayed?" Johnny asked, raising a brow.

"Yeah, I pray. Prayer saved my mom from cancer. Prayer's what you better learn to do if you want your mom to beat this."

Johnny laughed a little. "You pray? Yeah right."

Kent chuckled. "Yes, fool. Every day, all day. Even when I'm hanging with you."

Johnny frowned. "You? You act a fool all day, every day, and cuss like a sailor."

Kent grinned. "And I pray too. The streets are crazy, bro. You don't know what's gonna happen out here. And if you were praying, maybe, just maybe, things at home would be different."

Johnny looked down at his shoes. "Man, my mom prays all the time."

Kent's tone softened. "Yeah, but what about you? She can't carry this all by herself. She needs backup, man. I pray with my mom every night before bed: nine o'clock sharp. That's why I am in the house early. You think I'm scared of the dark? Nah, I just don't want my mom to worry. She's been through enough."

Johnny was quiet for a long moment.

Kent added, "Yo bro only got five years? That's because of your mom's prayers. My dad? They gave him thirty to life. He killed one of his pushers thinking they shorted him, plus the drug charges. He was ruthless. He was looking at life already."

Johnny let out a short laugh. "Thirty years? Man, that's crazy."

Kent nodded. "Yeah, but your mom's prayers. Those are strong. She probably saved GT's life too."

Johnny sighed. "Yeah, my mom used to pray with me all the time. But when she stopped, I stopped."

Kent was quiet for a moment. "Her prayers are not your prayers. Just because she stopped doesn't mean you had to."

Johnny frowned. "So now you are preaching to me?"

Kent chuckled. "Nah, bro. I'm just saying maybe you should start back. Especially now. Your mom needs it."

Johnny nodded slowly. "Yeah, you're right. I'm gonna jump in the shower and head to the hospital. Paula's there, I gotta relieve her so she can come home and get some rest."

"You want me to meet you up there? We can pray together if you want."

Johnny smiled faintly. "Yeah, I'd like that."

"Cool. I'll jump in the shower and let my mom know so she won't worry about me. See you there, bro."

Kent didn't hang up yet. "Hold up, bro. Before you go, I need you to hear me on this. Your mom needs more than just visits. She needs soldiers. You can't just stand by and watch her fight for her life. You gotta fight too."

Johnny was quiet, staring at the floor. "I don't know if I got it in me, Kent. I'm angry. At my dad, at everything...even at God sometimes."

Kent's voice softened. "Then tell Him that, bro. God can handle your anger. You think I ain't mad about my pops doing life? You think I ain't asking God why? But I still get down on my knees every night, because if I don't, the streets gon' eat me alive."

Johnny's throat tightened. "So you think praying will really change things for my mom?"

Kent didn't hesitate. "Yes. Prayer changes everything. You know that better than me. Your momma taught me how to pray back when we were kids."

Johnny let out a small laugh through his nose. "Yeah, she always made sure we said our prayers before bed."

Kent's tone turned firm. "Then be the man she raised. She's still fighting, John John. Don't let her fight alone. The Bible says, 'The prayer of a righteous person has great effectiveness.'"

Johnny repeated the words slowly, like he was trying to memorize them. "The effectual...fervent prayer of a righteous man..."

"That's right," Kent said. "Get back in the fight. Pray for your mom like your life depends on it 'cause it does. This ain't just about her healing. This is about your family surviving this."

Johnny swallowed hard. "Yeah...yeah, you're right. I'm gonna start tonight."

"That's what I wanted to hear." Kent's tone brightened. "Alright, I'll meet you at the hospital. We'll pray together."

"Thanks, bro," Johnny said quietly. "I needed that."

"Anytime. And Johnny?"

"Yeah?"

"Don't just go to the hospital hoping for good news. Go believing for a miracle."

Johnny stood still for a long moment after hanging up. Kent's words echoed in his mind. Then he whispered to himself, almost like saying a vow:

"Lord, I don't know if I still know how to do this right, but I'm gonna try. Please don't let my mom die."

And for the first time in a long time, Johnny got down on his knees to pray.

"God...it's me. John John." His voice cracked, almost embarrassed. "I don't even know what to say anymore. It's been a long time since I prayed like this."

Tears streamed down his face. "Lord, I'm scared. I can't lose my mom. Please...please save her life. Please heal her body, Lord. Don't let her die like this. Don't let cancer take her. Don't let pain take her. Don't let depression take her. Please, God! I need my mom."

Johnny's chest heaved as he cried, but suddenly the words started to come faster, stronger.

"And God...I don't know why this is coming out of my mouth right now, but...I pray for my dad too." He clenched his fists, almost fighting the words. "I don't even want to pray for him, God, he's hurt my mom so bad. He hurt me. He hurt us all."

Johnny's voice broke, but he didn't stop. "But I can't hate him anymore. I forgive him. Lord, do something in his heart. Break him down if you got to, but save him. Make him the man he was supposed to be. Heal him too 'cause I think he's broken just like the rest of us."

The tears poured freely. "And heal our family, God. Don't let this be the end of us. Cover Paula, cover GT, cover all of us. Lord, I can't carry this anger any more. I will give it to you. I trust you. Please bring my mom home. Please let her live."

By the time Johnny said "Amen," he was on his face, weeping, but something inside of him felt lighter, like a weight had been lifted. Sometimes healing doesn't wait until the pain is gone. It comes when you finally lay your burdens at the feet of the One who can carry them.

Chapter 21

Paula walked into the house pulling off her sweater. She had already dropped her bookbag at the door. As she took one of her feet out of her shoes, Paula coughed.

"I need to take a shower. I was up all day and I feel sticky. Feel like I'm coming down with the flu," Paula admitted to herself as she walked to the bathroom.

She went toward the bathroom to start the shower. Before she could reach the door, somebody banged on the front door uncontrollably.

"Who is it?!"

"Rick! It's me, Rick."

"Wait one minute."

Rick continued to knock. Before Rick could knock the door down, Paula quickly opened it. She opened up to find Rick sweating profusely.

As he ran into the house, Paula asked, "What's wrong with you? Why are you knocking on the door like some nut?"

"Where's your father?"

"He's not here."

"Where's your brother?"

"He's not here either." Paula looked at Rick with a seductive grin. "Why…do you want to start back up where we finished last night." Paula grabbed his arm to move him closer, but Rick pulled away.

"Hell no! I don't want you touching me ever again."

"What do you mean you don't want me to touch you ever again?"

Rick grabbed Paula by the arm with his body full of rage. Rick's nails embedded into Paula's arm as he got madder and madder. Sweat rolled down his forehead while he breathed heavily in Paula's face.

"You know what you did to me. Did you know you ruined my life?

"What are you talking about?" Paula tried pulling away from Rick's grasp with her sweater hanging around her neck. She thought she could entice the older man, but it was clear he was not in the mood.

The more Paula tried to get away the more angry Rick got. "I should kill you, bitch."

Shocked by the way Rick spoke to her, Paula became afraid. She had never seen him like this. "Wait, what did I do?"

"You ruined my life...that's what you did. You ruined me for life." Rick growled at Paula as he backhanded her across the face. She stumbled onto the couch as Rick got on top of her. Rick grabbed her face as tears fell and Paula screamed. Fear took over her body. In his eyes, Paula was no longer sexy.

Desperate to understand why Rick suddenly turned on her, Paul begged for answers while Rick powered over her. "What did I do? Tell me what I did."

"I got my test result back today. Bitch, you killed me. You gave me a death sentence." Paula wiggled to get from under Rick on the burgundy leather couch.

"What are you talking about?" Paula shouted as Rick hit her again.

Petrified by Rick's anger, Paula shrieked out "Help me! Somebody, help me, please!"

As Paula screamed for help, GT and George walked up toward the front door and looked at each other. George turned the key in the door. Hearing Paula's scream sent his temper off immediately. When they walked into the house, GT and George saw Rick on top of Paula and rushed to the couch. George and GT pulled Rick off Paula. As her father fought for her, Paula was consoled by GT on the couch. She was bleeding from her mouth and nose. Her eyes were almost shut and she barely noticed that GT was the person holding her. Paula blinked to see that the arms around her were her brother's. She yanked away and began to put her sweater back on.

"Nigger, what is wrong with you?" George screamed at his old friend and pounded on his face making blood run from his mouth.

"You lost your mind? George beat Rick uncontrollably, swinging his words and his fist. "That's my daughter you're hitting. You lost your mind."

GT tried to grab his dad off Rick. But George was not finished. "Are you crazy? I'll kill you for putting your hands on my daughter."

George looked at Paula and jumped at Rick again while GT held him back. Paula moved from the couch to get out of the way but was shocked at the scene.

GT moved toward Rick confused about what was going on, "Now Uncle Rick, you need to explain and explain quickly." George was not interested in any answer. He leaped at Rick again.

Knowing he was going to lose a fight against George and GT, Rick pulled out a gun. "Go ahead George, I came prepared. I'm planning on killing this bitch."

"Before you do that you're going to have to kill me first." George's Louis Vuitton tee shirt fell back into place as he breathed quickly. He stood with his eyes on Rick.

"Right now old friend, I don't mind taking everybody's life. My life is ruined!

"What do you mean, your life is ruined?" For the first time in the evening, George remembered that Rick was his friend.

Everyone in the room stood still as Juanita entered the house. She saw Paula bleeding and ran over to her holding her. Rick's face was full of blood as he held the gun up at George.

"What's going on here? What's happening?"

"I'll tell you what is happening. The last couple of months I haven't been feeling well." Rick pointed the gun between George and GT in fear of their every move.

"What's that got to do with anything?" George's anger pulsed through him making him see red but he wanted to know what was going on.

"So, I went to the doctor and took some blood tests. Only to find out today that this bitch here gave me HIV." Rick pointed the gun at Paula.

"Wait a minute! The only way my daughter could give you something–means you and her–As he connected the dots, George jumped at Rick. Rick didn't move away but pulled out a second gun.

"Yes, me and her."

"Paula is the young freak you've been telling me about this entire time…"

Rick laughed, "Yeah! Your daughter is the freak. I have been banging her for three and a half years.

"Wait a minute, she was only fourteen when you– I mean you– You pervert!" Juanita screamed at Rick.

"Correction thirteen and a HALF!" Rick hoped to hurt everyone under the sound of his voice.

George looked at Paula, heartbroken and confused, "Why?"

Paula looked at GT, "Tell him why, GT."

With his eyes spanning the whole living room, George couldn't make sense of anything. "What are you asking GT for?"

The drunkenness that brought Rick to their home finally entered the room. "Your girl is a whore. I have been hitting this for years. Now she gave me AIDS." Rick stumbled but picked his guns back up.

George jumped at Rick again but GT pulled his dad back.

"Old friend, I don't want to kill you. But, I think I will have to once I put a bullet between your sweet diamond's eyes!"

Paula looked at Rick through her swollen eyes, "I don't have AIDS. I'm not HIV positive. You did not get it from me."

"You are the only person I have been with, sweetie."

George leaped at Rick again and Rick shot him in the leg.

"I warn you old friend, I am not playing with you." George grabbed his leg in pain.

"I do not have HIV. I do not have AIDS." Paula screamed in denial.

"But, I do." GT's voice made everyone look at him. Paula stared at her brother.

"What do you mean you are? What does that have to do with Paula and this asshole?" George was so confused and angry. He rocked with pain. GT backed away from George worried about what he might do.

"Oh my, Lord Jesus! Say it isn't so. Just say it isn't so." Jaunita cried, holding Paula tighter.

"If Paula has HIV, she got it from me." GT confessed. George yelled in despair. Paula screamed and cried. Rick's jaw dropped down.

"I knew it. I knew it. I knew it." Juanita murmured.

"Where is your God now, Momma? Where is he now?" George collapsed to his knees, punching the floor, screaming to heaven.

"Out the house...where you put him."

Another gunshot fired with screams.

When Paula opened her eyes, Juanita was laying in front of Paula with a gunshot wound to her chest. George rushed Rick and the gun went off once more. This time it was Rick who was shot and First Lady Floyd was holding the gun. George fell to his knees crying out to God.

Secrets destroy families. Sin leaves blood on every hand. And sometimes the truth...comes with a bullet. But this is only the beginning. The story isn't over yet. The smoke hasn't cleared, and the battle isn't finished. Will Juanita survive? Will Rick make it? What becomes of Jenny, George, Paula, and GT? The answers are coming and they will change everything. The next chapter of their lives is waiting...and you won't want to miss what happens next.

Epilogue

"The Fall and the Light"

The room was silent after the sound. That single, hollow crack that broke the night. Then came the stillness. The kind that doesn't come from peace, but from pain too deep to move.

Jenny's hand trembled. The gun slipped from her fingers and hit the floor with a dull thud. For a moment, there was no pain, only warmth. And then, darkness.

Somewhere far off, a voice called her name. "Jenny…Jenny…"

She opened her eyes to light. Colors swirled and soft air pressed against her skin. She reached out and touched something that shimmered. It felt like water and clouds all at once.

Her body was gone. But her soul…her soul was awake.

A figure stepped forward, hand extended, eyes kind. "Welcome," he said. "You've been sent to the place of decisions."

Jenny looked around, confusion flickering across her face. "Am I dead?"

He smiled. "No, child. Not dead. Just lost. And he's not done with you yet."

The sound of running water filled the air, and from the distance came the laughter of children playing, doves flying, the echo of peace. But Jenny could still feel the weight of her pain pressing against her chest.

"I don't understand," she whispered.

"You will," the voice said gently. "But first, you must go back home."

Jenny blinked. "Home?"

"Yes," came the answer. "To where it all began."

And before she could cry out, the light around her deepened. Jenny began to fall.

Afterword

Your Story Is Not Over

Many of the topics mentioned in this book are consider controversial, especially in Christian communities. That's exactly why I wrote this book.

If you or someone you know is struggling like Jenny to find hope and to see the next steps...You are not alone. Help is available right now.

If you are in crisis, thinking about suicide, or worried about someone else, please reach out for confidential support:

National Suicide and Crisis Lifeline (U.S.)

- Call or text 988 — available 24 hours a day, 7 days a week.

- You can also visit: 988lifeline.org for live chat and

additional resources.

- If you're outside the U.S., you can find international hotlines here: findahelpline.com, which lists trusted resources around the world.

Your life matters. Your story is not over.

Healing doesn't happen in silence. You don't have to face your pain alone. There are safe, confidential spaces available for you to speak, heal, and grow.

BetterHelp Online Counseling

- Visit www.betterhelp.com: Get matched with a licensed therapist online. 100% confidential | Accessible anytime | Financial aid available

Focus on the Family — Christian Counseling Line

- 1-855-771-HELP (4357) Available Monday–Friday, 9am–7pm EST. Free, faith-based counseling & referral services.

Remember: Reaching out for help is not weakness — it's the beginning of healing.

Prayer for the Reader

A moment of healing, reflection, and hope for every person who just turned the last page.

Heavenly Father, We come before You with hearts wide open, carrying every wound, every scar, and every secret that has ever tried to break us. We lift up every reader who has walked through pain — abuse, betrayal, rejection, and loss — and we declare Your healing power over their lives right now.

Lord, break every chain of shame and silence. Restore every broken heart. Heal every place that has been violated, used, or abused. Cover every family represented with Your mercy and wash away the stain of sin with the blood of Jesus.

We ask You to redeem every story, turn every tragedy into testimony, and transform every victim into a victor. Let forgiveness flow where bitterness tried to live, and let love rise where hatred tried to grow.

We declare over every reader: You will live and not die. Your story is not over. God has the final say.

In Jesus' mighty name we pray, Amen.

About the Author

Ellen Black-Pace is the Founder and CEO of *My Heart Is In His Hands Ministry*, an organization devoted to reviving the creative gifts of individuals through mentorship, performance, and spiritual support. Born in New Jersey and raised in North Carolina, Ellen's journey in the arts began early through writing, comedy, and drama. She has performed widely in churches, developed original characters, and built a reputation for her unique ability to inspire both laughter and tears.

As a Prophet of the Lord with a background in administration and creative ministry, Ellen created the **Creative Revival Program** to reach those—especially young people—whose creative dreams have been deferred or unrecognized. Her calling is to activate imagination, purpose, and healing through the power of faith and expression.

For more information or to contact the author:
Email: myheartisinhishandsministry.ebp@gmail.com
Phone: 484-610-6318
Website: www.myheartisinhishands.com

OUR MISSION:

At My Heart Is In His Hands Ministry, we are dedicated to empowering and nurturing the creative potential within our community. By providing resources, mentorship, and opportunities for growth, we help individuals transform deferred dreams into reality, inspire the use of dormant gifts, and create a supportive platform where artists can launch and thrive in their creative careers.

CONTACT US

📞 484 610 6318

🌐 myheartisinhishandsministry.ebp@gmail.com

www.ingramcontent.com/pod-product-compliance
Lightning Source LLC
Chambersburg PA
CBHW072011070526
44583CB00015B/1434